DRAFTING CONTRACTS

A Practical Guide to Transactional Practice

BEN L. FERNANDEZ

DRAFTING CONTRACTS
A Practical Guide to Transactional Practice

Ben L. Fernandez

Published by:

Vandeplas Publishing, LLC – August 2020

801 International Parkway, 5th Floor
Lake Mary, FL. 32746
USA

www.vandeplaspublishing.com

ISBN 978-1-60042-516-5

DEDICATION

I dedicate this book to the most talented, supportive and collegial group of people I have ever worked with: Laura Rosenbury, Amy Mashburn, Silvia Menendez, Leslie Knight, Deborah Cupples, Margaret Temple-Smith, Kirsten Clement, Leigh Scales, Cynthia K. Stroud, Kirby Oberdorfer, and Susan K. Sloane.

CONTENTS

Preface

When I started to practice law more than thirty years ago, one of the first things I learned is that doing well in law school is very different than being successful in the practice of law. When I first started teaching legal drafting to law students I was again confronted by the fact that the skills needed to do well in my course were different than the skills needed to be successful in a transactional drafting practice. The average legal drafting course is really just a course on clear and organized writing. But there is much more to contract drafting than just writing.

In law school, the focus is on clarity and organization; the object is to make a contract as clear as possible by following a rigid set of rules for how to write different types of provisions and how to organize them. All the rules are mandatory. The students learn to draft a simple contract from scratch. They work alone and are graded on how close they can come to drafting a document with no "errors."

One of the rules is that students must be consistent. So, if the student writes, "the Seller <u>shall</u> paint the Building" and then adds "the Seller <u>will</u> only use white paint," the student loses a point for not being consistent. Another rule is to use active voice. So, if the student writes, "The building shall be painted by Contractor," the student loses a point for using passive voice.

In practice, the focus is on substance more than form. The facts aren't neatly packaged in an assignment memo; you have to interview the client to find out what the agreement is. And the client isn't just looking for you to just transcribe what he tells you; the lawyer is expected to add bring something extra to the table based on the lawyer's legal training and expertise.

In the classroom, students also draft alone. But in real life lawyers usually negotiate contract provisions with attorneys representing the other side. And the work isn't done when the writing is complete. Attorneys are also expected to close the deal, which typically involves getting the documents signed and collecting whatever funds are due.

I am writing this handbook to try to better bridge the gap between legal education and the practice of law. My objective is to cover what is taught in a typical transactional drafting course (drafting of obligations, rights, prohibitions and descriptive statements, as well as contract organization), but then supplement that material with a discussion of the type of work lawyers do in a transactional practice. You will learn to draft a simple agreement, but you will also work on making revisions to more complex documents because that's the type of work you will likely be doing if you practice in this area. And my goal is to give you enough information and advice that you can "hit the ground running" in a law firm or on your own after you have read this book.

Introduction

As an introduction to this material, consider the history of contract drafting and what it means for the role of attorneys in the drafting process. Every law student who has taken a first-year course on contracts law knows you don't need a lawyer to draft a simple contract. In fact, you don't need to put anything on paper; you don't even need to open your mouth. Since the beginning of time, mankind has been creating contracts without any legal education at all.

Imagine a Neanderthal roasting a buffalo over an open fire. As the meat cooks, he gorges himself until he can eat no more. Another Neanderthal approaches. He has been making spearheads all day and has nothing to eat. The first guy cuts off a piece of meat, holds it in one hand and points to one of the spear heads with the other hand (offer). Second guy hands the first guy a spear head, takes the meat and eats it (acceptance). Offer plus acceptance equals a contract.

Now think ahead in time to feudal England before there was paper. In those days, property was conveyed with a ceremony called the "livery of seisin." Here is a description of the ceremony from Bernulf Hodge in A History of Malmesbury:

> The lucky new Commoner goes to his "given" acre and cuts a turf from the selected site and drops two shillings in the hole made. The High Steward [of the County] then twitches him with a twig and sticks the twig in the turf, then hands it to him saying, "This turf and twig I give to thee, as free as Athelstan gave to me, and I hope a loving brother thou wilt be." The High Steward then takes the money out of the hole and the new landowner replaces the turf.

I don't know when they started using paper in England, but at some point, the practice changed, and people started writing things down. One of the earliest examples I can find of a written contract is an indentured servant agreement from the 1700's. This example of an early agreement is very simple and short, but the legalese is so intense it is hard to decipher the intent. If you want to understand why educators rail against legalese, try reading this document:

Indentured Servant Contract

This Indenture, Made the Fourth Day of August in the Twenty-ninth Year of the Reign of our Sovereign Lord George the Second King of Great Britain, And in the Year of our Lord, One Thousand Seven Hundred and fifty five Between William Buckland of Baford Carpenter & Joiner of the one Part, and Thomson Mason of London, Esq. of the other Part, Witnesseth, That the said William Buckland for the Consideration herein after-mentioned, hath, and by these Presents doth Covenant, Grant, and Agree to, and with the said Thomas Mason Executors and assigns, That He the said William Buckland shall and will, as a faithful Covenant Servant, well and truly serve the said Thomas Mason his Executors and assigns in the Plantation of Virginia beyond the Seas, for the Space of Four Years, next ensuing his Arrival in the said Plantation in the Employment of a Carpenter and Joiner. And the said William Buckland doth hereby Covenant and Declare himself, now to be the Age of Twenty two Years Single and no Covenant or contracted Servant to any other Person or Persons, And the said Thomas Mason for himself his Executors Or Assigns, in Consideration thereof, doth hereby Covenant, Promise And Agree to and with the said William Buckland his Executors, and Assigns, that He the said Thomas Mason his Executors or Assigns, shall and will at his or their own proper Costs and Charges, with what convenient Speed they may, carry and convey, or cause to be carried and conveyed over unto the said Plantation, the said William Buckland and from henceforth, and during the said Voyage, and also during the said Term, shall and will at the like Costs and Charges, provide for and allow the said William Buckland all necessary Meat, Drink, Washing, and Lodging, fit and convenient for William as Covenant Servants in such Cases are usually provided for and allowed and pay and allow William Buckland Wages on Salary at the Rate of Twenty Pounds Sterling per Annum Payable Quarterly And for the true Performance of the Premises, the said Parties, the these Presents bind themselves, their Executors and Administrators, the either to the other, in the Penal Sum of Forty Pounds Sterling, firmly by these Presents. In witness whereof, they have hereunto interchanged by set their Hands and Seals, the Day and Year above-written.

More modern contracts have benefitted from the "Plain English" movement, which describes a relatively recent trend in legal writing to make not just contracts, but also statutes and other documents, comprehensible to the average person.[1] One of the more universal tenets of that movement is the elimination of legalese. Also, law schools now routinely offer training in contract drafting. That training didn't exist thirty (30) years ago. As a result, many experienced drafters practicing today learned by doing, and draft in a hybrid style of plain language and legalese.

Today writing is more often recorded in digital form than on paper. And documents are sometimes signed online, not in person. When all that is required is to fill in the blanks in a simple form and e-mail it to someone to sign online, the process usually occurs without the help of an attorney. A computer can do that work much more efficiently. So, what is there for attorneys to do?

What attorneys are typically involved with are complex agreements governing situations where there is a lot at stake. Law students and new attorneys need to learn basic principles of how to draft contract provisions and organize them. They need to learn to pay close attention to language. And that is best taught in the context of a simple contract. But what you will ultimately spend most of your time doing is tailoring a form document for a specific deal; and when you are on the other side of a transaction, requesting revisions to a completed document to better protect the other side's interests. Also, you will have to deal with a host of other issues besides writing. The language in your documents will often be negotiated; and you will need to get the documents executed when you are done. There may be ethical issues you have to work out. And you will likely work with computers to get the process completed more efficiently. I want you to be as close as possible to "practice ready" by the time you finish reading this book. To do that I need to be make you familiar with all aspects of contract drafting, not just writing.

1 *See* Joseph Kimble, *Plain English: A Charter for Clear Writing*, 9 Thomas M. Cooley L. Rev. 1. (1992); Richard C. Wydick, *Plain English for Lawyers* (5th ed., Carolina Academic Press 2005). *See also* Shawn Burton, *The Case for Plain-Language Contracts*, Harvard Business Review (2018).

Chapter One
Getting up to Speed

The first step in contract drafting is getting up to speed. Before you even meet with the client to find out what the agreement is, you must prepare. And that means becoming familiar with the client's business and the nature of the goods or services involved, then conferencing with the client and flushing out the terms of the deal.

A. Become Familiar with the Goods or Services Involved

Suppose the client is hiring you to draft an agreement to construct a building. Do you know the process for constructing a building? Usually there is a set of "plans and specifications" that describe the structure. The plans, which are actually called "drawings," show the dimensions and location of each room; the specifications detail the materials to be used and the identity of things like appliances and furnishings. Then there is a budget itemizing how much everything will cost, and a schedule for when things will be done. Construction is not done by one person or entity; there is usually a "general contractor" who works with various "subcontractors" to get the work done. The people who pour the foundation are different than the people who do the framing. The electricians do the wiring and the plumbers do the piping. HVAC (heating, ventilation, and air conditioning) is handled by one group, and drywall is handled by another. The coordination and payment of all these parties is critical to the timely completion of the project.

If there are changes (and there usually are), there is a "change order" procedure that has to be gone through. If subcontractors don't get paid, there are "material men's liens" that have to be dealt with. And that process is usually governed by a state statute. If there is financing, the lender will constantly be verifying that the loan is "in balance" (i.e. there is enough money left to complete the project). If there is insurance, the insurer will also want to monitor construction progress, so that the amount of coverage can be adjusted as the building is constructed. At a minimum, you have to be familiar with all of these things before you meet with the client to learn the deal. If you don't do that preparation, communication with the client may be hampered. You may not be able to draft the contract well, and you may also cause the client to lose confidence in you. For a lawyer, that is the beginning of the end. You can't risk letting that happen.

Learn as much as you can about the client and the client's business before you meet. If you are not familiar with the product or service that will be involved in the agreement, take the time to get up to speed. Learn the lingo so you can understand what the client is telling you. Make sure you are familiar with any laws or regulations that might apply to the contract, the subject matter or the business involved. The client will be expecting you to have that familiarity and may ask you about those issues. If you can at least give the impression that you know what you are doing, the client will have confidence in you, and the process will be facilitated. Before you do just about anything as an attorney, you must first prepare.

B. FLUSH OUT THE TERMS OF THE DEAL

The second step is to meet with the client and find out the terms of the deal. And the first thing to know about that step is that most people don't like meeting with lawyers. I know it's hard to imagine, but for the average person, going to see a lawyer is like going to the dentist. You know you have to do it, but you don't want to, and you hope to get it over with as soon as possible. For lawyers that means it isn't always easy to get the client to sit down and go through all the facts of the deal with you. So, make the process as painless as possible. Have a list of questions or an outline ready. Ask open ended questions, like you would in a deposition (i.e. questions that begin with who, what, where, when, why, and how). Listen carefully and take good notes.[2]

2 My impression is that some people think the advent of the personal computer, and specifically the lightweight laptop, has eliminated the need for note taking; but that is a critical mistake. Note taking has traditionally been done with pen and paper, that's true. Now most writing is done on a computer, that's true too. But that does not mean taking notes is old-fashioned. If you insist on not carrying pen and paper, you must take notes just as accurately and completely on your laptop (assuming your client doesn't think it's rude for you to be staring at a computer screen while she's talking). If you don't, you will lose out on higher grades in school and profitable business opportunities in practice. No sophisticated client will tolerate you relying on memory in an important business meeting, like an initial conference to discuss deal terms.

What you want is to get to the point where you know everything the client knows. Who agreed to what? What did the other guy agree to in exchange? What else was agreed upon? What representations were made? You may be surprised to find there are a lot of things that weren't discussed but should have been. Keep track of what those things were. And keep asking questions until you have completely flushed out all the elements of the deal, and all the details of each element. There will come a time when you actually know the deal better than the client. But for now, just make sure you know everything the client knows. Also, try to establish a rapport with the client; and leave the door open when you are done. After the next step you will need to talk to him or her again.

Those are the two steps to getting up to speed. Make yourself familiar with the goods or services involved before you meet with the client. That will facilitate the second step, which is flushing out all the terms of the deal. Once you have done those two things, you should have everything you need to start drafting.

Chapter Two

Drafting covenants, rights, prohibitions, and descriptive statements

Contracts typically contain four types of provisions: covenants, rights, prohibitions, and descriptive statements. Covenants are provisions that obligate a party to do something in the future he wasn't already obligated to do. Rights are provisions that give a party the right to do something in the future he didn't already have the right to do. Prohibitions prohibit a party from doing something he would otherwise have had the right to do. And descriptive statements, including representations and warranties and policy statements, are statements of circumstances that existed in the past or on the date the contract was executed.

What is most important in drafting these provisions is making sure they are clear and unambiguous. Clarity is typically achieved by keeping the sentence structure simple, and making your factual references accurate and precise. Clarity is also achieved by being consistent: doing the same types of provisions the same way every time.[3] In addition to making provisions clear and unambiguous, it is also important to make sure they are complete. To do that, ask what a colleague of mine used to refer to as the "w" questions: "who," "what," "to whom," "where," "when," and "how," as applicable. Not all of those questions will apply to every covenant, but you should have answers to as many of them as do apply. Those are the basic principles you need to follow when drafting covenants, rights, prohibitions and descriptions.

3 When Ralph Waldo famously said "a foolish consistency is the hobgoblin of little minds" it wasn't contract drafting he was referring to. Ralph Waldo Emerson, Self-Reliance (1841). Consistency is the most important tenet of clear drafting. If you draft a covenant to read "the Seller shall sell the Property to the Buyer," then you should draft all your covenants the same way (i.e. using the word "shall"). If you write in the agreement the contractor shall provide his own "tools, materials, and supplies," then you should use that phrase and only that phrase every time you describe what the contractor is required to provide. Be consistent!

A tenant's obligation to pay rent to a landlord is an example of a covenant. To make it clear a covenant is intended, use plain English, keep the sentence structure simple, and use the same wording every time. Start with the name of the party you are assigning the obligation to; and just state what the person agreed to do. Don't say "the Tenant doth covenant and agree to pay the rent." Say instead:

The Tenant will pay the rent.

In English a future tense statement is created using the word "will" or "shall" prior to the applicable verb. Use plain English and create contract covenants the same way.

As between "will" and "shall" many practitioners find "shall" is easiest to use, and, for that and other reasons, "shall" is probably used most often in modern contracts.[4] I personally think "shall" sounds old fashioned. It's not a word I would otherwise use in my writing, so I don't use it in contracts either. In this handbook, all the examples of covenants are written using "will."

In addition to consistently using the same wording, you should also make sure your obligations are complete. That is accomplished by asking yourself "who" are you assigning the obligation to, "what" does that person have to do, "to whom" will performance be provided, "when" is performance due, and "how" is it to be accomplished. And then make the covenant accurate by answering those questions exactly as the client answered them.

So, for example, if you were drafting a covenant to pay rent, you would start by asking who you are obligating to pay the rent.

---

4 There is much scholarly debate in the literature about which word is better: "shall" or "will." *E.g.*, Chadwick C. Busk, *Using Shall or Will to Create Obligations in Business Contracts*, Mich. Bar J. (2017). Some of the leading scholars in this area argue "shall" is better. *E.g.*, Kenneth A. Adams, *A Manual of Style for Contract Drafting* (4th ed. 2017), Tina L. Stark, *Drafting Contracts: How and Why Lawyers Do What They Do* (2d ed. 2007). Others prefer "will." Brian A. Garner, *Guidelines for Drafting and Editing Contracts* (1st ed. 2019), Barbara Child, *Drafting Legal Documents: Materials and Problems* (2d ed. 1988). My position is either is fine as long as you are consistent. *E.g.*, Margaret Temple-Smith and Deborah Cupples, *Legal Drafting: Litigation Documents, Contracts, Legislation, and Wills* (1st ed. 2012).

The Tenant

Then add the word "will" since this is a covenant.

The Tenant will

Ask yourself, the Tenant will what?

The Tenant will pay rent

To whom will the rent be paid?

The Tenant will pay rent to the Landlord

How much is the rent?

The Tenant will pay rent to the Landlord in the amount of five hundred dollars ($500)

When is the rent due?

On or before the first day of each month, the Tenant will pay rent to the Landlord in the amount of five hundred dollars ($500)

How is the rent to be paid?

On or before the first day of each month, the Tenant will pay rent to the Landlord in the amount of five hundred dollars ($500) by check or money order.

Assuming the rent actually is $500 per month, you have now drafted a clear, complete, and accurate covenant requiring the tenant to pay the rent.

When you are drafting covenants make sure you avoid obligating the parties to come to an agreement in the future, like this:

> The Landlord and the Tenant will agree on an appropriate late charge.

An agreement to agree is generally not enforceable. Plus, the whole idea of drafting a contract is to help the parties to come to an agreement now, and then put that agreement in writing.

B. DRAFT RIGHTS USING "MAY"

A landlord's right to conduct periodic inspections of the property is an example of a contract right. To make it clear a right is intended, use plain English, keep the sentence structure simple, and use the same wording every time. Start with the party's name, then state what the person "may" do. Use the word "may" and only the word "may" every time you give someone the right to do something. Make sure the provision is complete by asking yourself "who," "what," "to whom," "when," and "how," as applicable. As long as your end result reflects what the client wanted, you are all set.

For example, if you were drafting a right to inspect an apartment, you would start by asking to whom are you are granting that right?

> The Landlord

Add the word "may" since this is a grant of rights.

> The Landlord may

May do what?

The Landlord may inspect the Unit

When?

The Landlord may inspect the Unit on any weekday between the hours of 9:00 a.m. and 5:00 p.m.

How?

The Landlord may inspect the Unit on any weekday between the hours of 9:00 a.m. and 5:00 p.m., if the Landlord gives notice

Gives notice to whom?

The Landlord may inspect the Unit on any weekday between the hours of 9:00 a.m. and 5:00 p.m., if the Landlord gives notice to the Tenant

When does the notice have to be given?

The Landlord may inspect the Unit on any weekday between the hours of 9:00 a.m. and 5:00 p.m., if the Landlord gives notice to the Tenant at least twenty-four hours before the proposed inspection.

By following the suggested protocols, you have now drafted a grant of rights that is clear, complete, and accurate.

There are a couple things to avoid when using the word "may." The first is to avoid giving someone the right to do something they already have the right to do, like this:

The Tenant may request that the term of the Lease be extended.

The Tenant can request whatever the Tenant wants to request. It is not necessary to give the Tenant the right to do something he already has the right to do.

The second is to avoid characterizing an obligation as a right. If you want the Tenant to return the keys to the property, do it like this:

> The Tenant will return the keys to the Property.

Not like this:

> The Landlord may receive the keys to the Property.

Among other things, if the Tenant doesn't return the keys, you want to be able to enforce a provision of the Lease obligating the Tenant to return them. A Lease provision saying the Landlord has the right to receive the the keys will be of no use to you.

C. DRAFT PROHIBITIONS USING "WILL NOT"

A provision a provision taking away the tenant's right to have pets in the unit is an example of a prohibition. To make it clear a prohibition is intended, just say what the person "will not" do; and consistently use those words every time you express a prohibition.[5] Do not use "may not."

If you were drafting a prohibition against pets, for example, you would start by asking who you are prohibiting.

> The Tenant

Add the words "will not" since this is a prohibition.

5 If you are using "shall" for covenants, then use "shall not" for prohibitions.

The Tenant will not

Will not do what?

The Tenant will not have pets

Where?

The Tenant will not have pets in the Unit

When?

The Tenant will not have pets in the Unit at any time during the Term.

Think of the Ten Commandments in the Bible. When Moses came down from the mountain, he didn't say "Thou shalt not kill." "Thou may not commit adultery." "Thou must not steal." "Thou will not bear false witness against thy neighbor." "Coveting thy neighbor's goods shall not be done either." He didn't mix it up. He did every prohibition the same way every time. When you draft prohibitions, you should do the same thing.

The primary thing to avoid when using "will not" is using that phrase for what are really descriptive statements. If the agreement is for the tenant to have free access to the exercise room, don't draft the applicable provision like this:

The Tenant will not pay for access to the exercise room.

You don't need to prohibit the tenant from paying for that access. You just need to make clear she doesn't have to pay for that access, like this:

The Tenant's access to the exercise room is provided free of charge.

D. DRAFT DESCRIPTIONS USING PAST OR PRESENT TENSE STATEMENTS

The other types of provisions you will find in contracts are descriptions. They are simply past or present tense statements describing factual information. If you think future tense is appropriate, try substituting a present tense statement. For example, instead of "any oral amendment of this Agreement will be invalid," say "any oral amendment of this Agreement is invalid."

Examples of descriptive statements include the exordium and testimonium[6] of a contract, as well as the background section. For example, if you wanted to describe a landlord's business, you might do it like this:

> The Landlord owns and manages over 1,000 rental properties in Northern Central Florida.

A statement of duration or term is another example of a descriptive statement. And the policy provisions typically included at the end of agreements can be drafted as descriptive statements too. For example, instead of saying "the parties will file any litigation arising out of this Agreement only in Alachua County," you would say "Alachua County is the mandatory and exclusive venue for litigation arising out of this Agreement."[7]

Representations and warranties are descriptive statements too. When you draft a representation and warranty, it is important to state who is making the statement and to whom it is being made, like this:

> The Tenant represents and warrants to the Landlord that the information in the Rental Application is accurate and truthful.

Representations and warranties actually serve two functions. One is to create a default if it turns out the information isn't true. If the tenant in the above

6 The exordium is the introductory paragraph in a contract; and the testimonium is the concluding paragraph prior to the signature lines. Both these sections are explained in more detail in the sections on organization in this handbook.

7 Statements of duration and policy statements are also covered in the sections on organization in this handbook.

example lies on his application, and the landlord finds out, the relationship can be ended. The other is sometimes called an "audit function." When you ask a corporation to represent that it is duly organized and existing, what you really want is for the corporation's lawyer to check and make sure the corporation has been following all the required corporate formalities before the document is signed. In other words, you add the representation so the other party will check and make sure it's true before the document is signed.

The differences between a representation and warranty and any other descriptive statement are the following: (1) a representation and warranty is a statement that is relied on by the other party to enter into the agreement; and (2) the other party has the right to end the relationship or otherwise back out of the deal if it turns out the representation and warranty is not true. So if one party wants a purchase and sale agreement to say the house was the boyhood home of former president George Washington, then that should be a representation and warranty. But if the parties to a broker's agreement want to make clear one the broker is an independent contractor, that should just be a descriptive statement.

The hard part for a novice draftsperson is not so much drafting the provision correctly, it is recognizing when something the client tells you is a covenant, when it is a right, when it is a prohibition, and when it is a descriptive statement. Whenever one party wants to obligate another party to do something in the future, whether they use the words "agrees to," or "is responsible for," or "promises," you should translate the wording to "will." Whenever one party gives another party the right to do something in the future, whether they use the words "can" or "has discretion to," you should translate the wording to "may." And when one party wants to prohibit another party from doing something, whether they use the words "can't," "may not," or "prohibit," you should translate the wording to "will not." Everything else is likely a descriptive statement. Draft them using the past or present tense. Draft your covenants, prohibitions, and rights consistently in this way to make your contract provisions as clear as possible.

Chapter Three
Avoiding Potentially Ambiguous Words and Phrases

In addition to consistently drafting covenants, rights, prohibitions, and descriptive statements, there are a number of potentially ambiguous words and phrases you need to avoid. Using "months" or the word "within" in time periods can make them unclear. Misplacing time periods and dates in conditions can also create ambiguity. You need to know what a "false obligation" is, and what passive voice is, so you can avoid both in contracts. You should also leave legalese and gender pronouns out of your agreements. And you should spell out numbers too, especially when you are referring to large dollar amounts.

A. Make Clear the Trigger Date, Duration, and End Date for Time Deadlines

Time deadlines are difficult to write clearly. You may not have thought about it, but a statement like "the Contractor will pay the Subcontractor within one (1) month" is rife with ambiguity. One month from when? The statement doesn't say when the clock starts ticking. Which month? February has twenty-eight days; January has thirty-one days. Does the period vary depending on when it starts? Also, can the Subcontractor pay on the last day or does he have to pay before the last day? There is no clear answer to any of those questions.

There are three things you should address when you draft a time deadline like this. First, use language that clearly indicates whether payment can happen on the last day or if it must be received before the last day, like "on or before," "on or after," "no later than," or "at least." So, you would start like this:

> The Contractor will pay the Subcontractor on or before

Rather than use months to describe the time period (or even weeks), it is preferable to use days. Why? Because every day is twenty-four hours long, no matter which day it is. So, draft it like this:

> The Contractor will pay the Subcontractor on or before the thirtieth (30th) day

And don't forget to include the date the period starts to run. Some practitioners refer to that as the "trigger date."

> The Contractor will pay the Subcontractor on or before the thirtieth (30th) day after the Project is completed.

Now that is much clearer than "The Contractor will pay the Subcontractor within one (1) month."

B. DON'T "SANDWICH" THE TIME PERIOD IN CONDITIONS

Conditions are also common in agreements. Drafting them is no different than the way you would do it normally (use "if" and "then," "unless" or "except"). A covenant can be subject to a condition, a grant of rights can be subject to a condition, and a prohibition can be subject to a condition. For example, failing to pay timely is usually the condition to incurring a late fee:

> If the Tenant fails to timely pay rent to the Landlord, then the Tenant will pay the Landlord a late fee in the amount of $25.00.

That is simple enough. But when you add a time period to a condition, you may inadvertently create ambiguity in your document if you don't put it in the right place. Here is an example:

If the Tenant fails to timely pay rent to the Landlord, on or before the fifth (5th) day of the month, the Tenant will pay the Landlord a late fee in the amount of $25.00.

Does the Tenant have to pay the rent on or before the fifth day of the month? Or does the Tenant have to pay the late fee on or before the fifth day of the month? The provision is ambiguous because the time deadline is "sandwiched" right in between the two phrases. It could apply to the first phrase or it could apply to the second phrase. To resolve this ambiguity, make sure you put the time deadline within the phrase to which it applies, like this:

If the Tenant fails to timely pay rent to the Landlord, the Tenant will pay the Landlord a late fee in the amount of $25.00 on or before the fifth (5th) day of the month.

This principle applies to modifiers generally. A modifier is a word or phrase in a sentence that modifies another word or phrase. If you misplace a modifier, the result is an ambiguous sentence. To rectify that issue, remember to always place the modifier as close as possible to the word or phrase it modifies.

C. DON'T OMIT THE PARTY FROM OBLIGATIONS, RIGHTS AND PROHIBITIONS

Make sure you don't leave the party out of your obligations, rights and prohibitions. In other words, don't write: "The house will have a concrete foundation." If you are drafting a covenant, you need to say who you are obligating to do the work. If you don't, you have created what's called a "false obligation." The obligation is there but it isn't given to anyone. To rectify that issue, you would instead say "the Builder will construct the house with a concrete foundation." If you are drafting an obligation, right, or prohibition, start with the name of the party you are obligating, empowering, or prohibiting. And then, you won't have to worry about creating false obligations.

D. DON'T OBLIGATE, PROHIBIT, OR EMPOWER PEOPLE WHO ARE NOT PARTIES TO THE CONTRACT

Make sure you don't include non-parties in your obligations, rights, and prohibitions. For example, if your contract is between a Contractor and a Subcontractor, don't draft a covenant that purports to obligate employees of the Subcontractor to do something. The employees are not parties to the contract. Rather, obligate the Subcontractor to instruct its employees to do something or obligate the Subcontractor to ensure that they do it. So, don't write "Employees of the Subcontractor will obtain adequate training before operating the Equipment." Write something like "the Subcontractor will adequately train the Subcontractor's employees before permitting them to use the Equipment."

E. AVOID PASSIVE VOICE; USE ACTIVE VOICE

Avoid passive voice when drafting contract provisions. If you write "the house will be painted red by the Seller," you are putting the focus on the house. But that's not what you want to do. You want to put the focus on the Seller, not the house. You are assigning the obligation to a person not a thing. And you do that by using active voice. In other words, you do that by writing it this way: "the Seller will paint the house red." Again, if you are drafting an obligation, right, or prohibition, start with the name of the party you are obligating, empowering, or prohibiting; and you should be fine.

The only exception to this rule I can think of is for the exordium and the testimonium. When drafting either of those descriptive statements, it is acceptable to put the focus on the document, not the parties, since both of those statements describe the execution of the document itself, not the provisions of the agreement between the parties.

F. AVOID LEGALESE; USE MODERN ENGLISH

Avoid using legalese in a modern business agreement. We don't wear powdered wigs anymore. We don't go to work on horseback. And no one still has wooden teeth. The 1800's have come and gone. We should use the language of the age in which we practice. Neither clarity, nor completeness, nor accuracy is accomplished with phrases like "witnesseth," "whereas," "hereinafter," "now therefore," or "hereinbefore." Avoid using those archaic expressions in a modern document.

I know some lawyers would argue that adding just a little legalese here and there doesn't hurt anything and it makes the document look more "official." In other words, it's a matter of style. To be clear, if you are revising someone else's document that has legalese in it, I would not recommend that you go through the document and delete all the archaic expressions. But when you draft from scratch, you should leave the legalese out.

Remember the Indentured Servant Agreement? Here it is without the legalese and applying the protocols I have gone through so far:

Indentured Servant Contract

On August 4, 1755, William Buckland (Buckland) and Thomson Mason (Mason) agree as follows:

1. Buckland will serve Mason in the Plantation of Virginia for the term of four years as a carpenter and joiner.
2. Buckland represents to Mason that Buckland is twenty-two years old, single, and not contracted to serve any other person.
3. Mason will, at his own cost, carry and convey Buckland to the Plantation.
4. Mason will, at his own cost, provide necessary meat, drink, washing, and lodging for Buckland.
5. Mason will pay Buckland wages at the rate of twenty pounds sterling per annum payable quarterly.

Executed as of the date above.

That is much clearer than it was, isn't it? It turns out the agreement was very simple and straight forward. But the legalese so obscured the meaning that it was difficult to see what the parties had agreed to.

G. AVOID GENDER PRONOUNS; REPEAT PARTY NAMES

I would also recommend that you avoid gender specific pronouns like "he," "she," "his," and "hers" in your contracts. If you use them in a provision in a form document, like this: "the Broker will perform his duties to the satisfaction of the Seller," you are going to have to remember to change "his" to "her" every time the gender of the broker changes. Or you could have one set of forms for men and another set for women. But the preferred method would be to get into the habit of not using the pronouns at all, like this: "the Broker will perform the Broker's duties to the satisfaction of the Seller." Do that and you won't have to worry about checking all your pronouns every time you draft a document.

Another reason to omit pronouns is because they can be a source of ambiguity if not used properly. If you write a sentence like this: "The Contractor will arrange for delivery of the Equipment to the Subcontractor, at his sole cost and expense" it is unclear whether "his" refers to the Contractor or the Subcontractor. To clarify this issue, omit the pronoun, like this: "The Contractor will arrange for the delivery of the Equipment to the Subcontractor, at the Contractor's sole cost and expense."

H. WRITE NUMBERS OUT

You have probably noticed I have been drafting numbers by writing them out, then putting the numeral in parenthesis. There is a simple reason that practitioners do it that way, and that is because it is harder to make a mistake when you write it out. Writing $100,000 instead of $1,000,000 seems like a relatively minor typo. I just left out one of the zeros. But that little typo could translate to a $900,000 malpractice claim. Spelling plaintiff with three (3) f's in an appellate brief, might cause a little damage to your reputation, but doing that will not likely cause any monetary harm. Typos involving numbers in contracts, especially big dollar numbers, can have a direct adverse monetary impact on the drafter. That is why it is usually advisable to spell numbers out, especially large dollar amounts, like you would if you were writing a check. So, instead of writing $100,000, get into the habit of doing it like this:

One hundred thousand and 00/100 dollars ($100,000.00).

In summary, pay a little extra attention to time periods to make sure you articulate them clearly. Be clear what the trigger date is, how long the duration is in days, and whether the last day is included. Make sure you understand what passive voice is, so you can avoid it in your documents. Don't leave the party out of obligations, rights, and prohibitions; and don't put nonparties in obligations, rights, and prohibitions. Use modern English, not legalese. Leave gender out of business documents. Make sure modifiers are as close as possible to the words or phrases they modify, especially when you articulate a condition. And watch out for numbers in particular. Lawyers are trained to pay close attention to language, but it is the numbers that can really get you into trouble.[8]

Now that we have covered how to clearly and unambiguously draft covenants, right, prohibitions and descriptive statements, and what potentially ambiguous words and phrases to avoid, we will next talk about how to organize the provisions of a contract. Sentences are made clear by keeping them simple, accurately and precisely describing factual information, and drafting the same provisions the same way. A contract is made clear by grouping and ordering the contract's provisions in an organized way. That is the subject of the next few chapters.

8 I included a "Flowchart for Drafting Contract Provisions" at the end of this handbook. If you have difficulty with this topic, try using the flowchart to work your way through each provision of the contract you are drafting.

Practice Exercises

Translate the following facts into appropriate contract provisions using the protocols in Chapters 2 and 3.

1. The manufacturer is going to make electric scooters for the school. The scooters will be speed limited to 35 mph. $1,000 will be paid by the school for each scooter; 48 will be sold.
2. Payment is due 6/5/2019. Wire transfer will be used for payment.
3. The school also promises to pay a fee of $35. But this only applies if payments are late.
4. Repair and maintenance services will be provided by the manufacturer. The school just has to notify the manufacturer in writing if the services are needed.
5. Rent is $250 per month due on the first day of every month. If the tenant doesn't pay on time, the tenant will have to pay interest on the payment at the rate of 1% per day.
6. The employee told the employer she was licensed to practice law in Florida. The employer relied on the representation in hiring her.
7. The school is prohibited from selling scooters to non-students.
8. The manufacturer can sell to students, but they can't charge students more than $1,000 per scooter.
9. The subcontractor is not allowed to put a sign on the site.
10. The employer can terminate the employment, if the employee tests positive for illegal drugs.
11. The employee is not allowed to solicit business from the employer's clients.
12. The landlord has the right to inspect the apartment. But the landlord has to first notify the tenant.
13. The tenant can use the pool, but he has to get a pool pass first.
14. Consent is required to sublet the apartment. But the landlord agrees that it will not unreasonably withhold consent.
15. Notice will be provided by the tenant within a month after the lease ends.

Answers to Practice Exercises

1. The manufacturer will make forty-eight scooters and sell them to the school. The manufacturer will make the scooters speed limited to 35 mph. The school will buy the scooters from the manufacturer and pay the manufacturer $1,000 per scooter for a total of $48,000.
2. On or before June 5, 2019, the school will pay the manufacturer for the scooters. The school will pay by wire transfer.
3. If any payment is late, the school will also pay the manufacturer a late fee of thirty-five dollars ($35).
4. The manufacturer will provide the school with repair and maintenance services, if the school notifies the manufacturer in writing that such services are needed.
5. On or before the first day of each month, the tenant will pay the landlord rent in the amount of two hundred fifty dollars ($250). If the tenant pays late, the tenant will also pay the landlord a late fee in the amount of one percent (1%) of the rent payment for every day the rent is paid late.
6. The employee represents and warrants to the employer that the employee is licensed to practice law in Florida.
7. The school will not sell scooters to non-students.
8. The manufacturer may sell the scooters to students. However, the manufacturer will not charge students more than one thousand dollars ($1,000) per scooter.
9. The subcontractor will not place a sign on the site.
10. The employer may terminate the employment, if the employee tests positive for illegal drugs.
11. The employee will not solicit business from the employer's clients.
12. If the landlord notifies the tenant first, the landlord may inspect the apartment.
13. If the tenant gets a pool pass, the tenant may use the pool
14. The tenant may sublet the apartment with the landlord's consent. The landlord will not unreasonably withhold consent.
15. The tenant will provide notice to the landlord no later than the thirtieth (30th) day after the lease ends.

Chapter Four
Organizing a Contract's Beginning Sections

Agreements typically start with a title, then an introductory paragraph that identifies the parties, the document, and the date. There is no requirement to include a background section, but it is often helpful to include one. In a short document, definitions are usually created in context; but in a longer document, when you have a lot of definitions, it is often advisable to include a definitions section. The same is true of representations and warranties. If you have a lot, it would be best to create a section for them and put the section near the beginning of the agreement.

A. Identify the Type of Agreement in the Title

Contracts typically start with a title describing the type of agreement involved. If you are drafting a lease agreement for the rental of a residential apartment, don't just title it "Agreement." That doesn't distinguish it from any other agreement. And don't write a title that goes too far in the other direction, like this: "Agreement between Landlord Corp. and Tammy Tenant Concerning the Rental of the Apartment at 123 Main Street in Gainesville, Florida." That's too much information. Most of it belongs in the body of the agreement, not the title. Just identify the type of agreement, like this:

APARTMENT LEASE

I capitalized, centered, and underlined the title to make it stand out. You can also use bold to make a title (or a heading) stand out in an agreement (or some other combination of one or more of those four techniques). But don't do things like italicizing letters, making the font bigger, or using any type of graphics. That will just make the agreement look tacky. Keep it professional!

B. START WITH AN EXORDIUM (PREAMBLE OR INTRODUCTION)

After the title there should be an introductory section called the "exordium."[9] The exordium is a description of what the parties are doing (entering into a contract). It contains the date of the agreement, the identity of the parties, and the title of the document, as well as short-hand references for the parties and the document. There are two ways to do it. One is passive voice and puts the emphasis on the document, like this:

> This Apartment Lease (Lease) is entered into on this ___ day of __________, 20___, by and between Landlord Corp., a Florida corporation, having an office at 57 West Street, Gainesville, Florida (Landlord) and Tammy Tenant of 75 First Street, Gainesville, Florida (Tenant).

The other is active voice and puts the emphasis on the parties, like this:

> On ________________ _____, 20_____, Landlord Corp., a Florida corporation, having an office at 57 West Street, Gainesville, Florida (Landlord) and Tammy Tenant of 75 First Street, Gainesville, Florida (Tenant) enter into this Apartment Lease (Lease).

I personally prefer the active voice form, but many attorneys also use the other one. What is important in drafting an exordium is not so much the form you use, but the information you include and the way you express that information. To identify a person, you need the person's full name and address. To identify an entity like a corporation, you need the entity's name and address, but you also need to know the state in which the entity was organized. This information is important for a number of reasons.

First and foremost, a contract entered into with the wrong party or something that is not an actual party, is worthless. If you start a real estate purchase agreement by stating "Lancaster Williams" is the seller, but title to the property is actually held by "Lancaster Family Trust," you have made a serious mistake. If you are drafting an agreement for the purchase of business assets and you state

9 "Exordium" is Latin for "a beginning" or "commencement." Lewis & Short, *Latin Dictionary.*

the seller is "Frannie's Pizza," your contract is no good. "Frannie's Pizza" may be the name of the business but it is not a person or entity. You must state the name of the owner, Frannie Salpietro, and then you can add "d/b/a Frannie's Pizza."

Second, you must include addresses to enable the parties to provide notice to each other. A loan agreement may require a lender to give a borrower notice of default, so it is helpful if the agreement says where the borrower is located. If the same agreement is breached and the lender wants to sue the borrower, it will, again, be helpful to know where the borrower can be served with the summons and complaint.

When you draft the exordium, you must express this information accurately. Make sure you have the party names correct. Also, when you refer to the document the parties are entering into, make sure you describe it accurately. Don't say the parties "enter into this rental agreement" if you have titled the contract "apartment lease." State the parties "enter into this apartment lease."

After the exordium, you need to insert what are called "words of agreement." In older agreements, you would do that by saying something like "Now, therefore, in consideration of the mutual covenants herein contained, the parties agree as follows" or "Now, therefore, for good and valuable consideration the sufficiency of which is hereby acknowledged, the parties agree to the following." But today the preferred practice is to leave out the legalese and the recitation of consideration and just add the following sentence to the end of the exordium: "The parties mutually agree as follows." Alternatively, If a background section is included (discussed below), it is common to add "Accordingly, the parties agree as follows" after the background section. Either way is fine.

C. CONSIDER INCLUDING A BACKGROUND SECTION

After the exordium you may want to include a background section. A contract does not have to have a background section, but it is often helpful to include one. For example, you may want to explain the events that led up to the creation of the contract or the context within which the contract is signed. If you are drafting an employment agreement, you could do something like this:

I. Background of Agreement

A. The Employer conducted a nationwide search for qualified trial attorneys by posting an advertisement in the journal of the American Bar Association.

B. The Employee responded to the advertisement by submitting a current resume listing the Employee's education, employment and outside affiliations (Resume), a true and accurate copy of which is attached to this Agreement as Exhibit A.

C. The Employer interviewed the Employee and offered the Employee employment; and the Employee accepted the offer.

I used this section to authenticate the employee's resume, and I created a short-hand term for that document. I did that so I would have a simple but accurate way to refer to the resume in the body of the agreement. For example, I might want the employee to represent to the employer that the statements in the Resume are truthful. If it turns out the employee was lying, that would constitute a breach, enabling the employer to end the relationship.

Another reason you may want to do a background section is to describe the parties and the subject matter of the agreement. For example, if you were drafting an equipment lease, you might do something like this:

I. Background of Agreement

A. Business of Food Service Corp. Food Service Corp. is in the business of operating food service kiosks in shopping malls in Northern Central Florida.

B. Equipment for Kiosks. Food Service Corp. has determined that it is in its best interests to lease, rather than purchase the kitchen equipment for its food kiosks.

C. Business of Supply Corp. Supply Corp. is in the business of leasing commercial kitchen equipment to restaurants and other food service providers in Florida.

D. Equipment for Lease. This Agreement concerns the following pieces of equipment: one Vulcan VC44GD - Double Deck Gas Convection Oven, Mfg Part#: VC44GD, one Anets SLG100 - Commercial Gas Fryer, 70 to 100 Lb. Oil Capacity, Mfg Part#: SLG100, one True T-49F - Commercial Freezer - Two Door - Reach-In - 49 Cu. Ft., Mfg Part#: T-49F-HC and three Kratos TT-244 - Stainless Steel Work Tables with Galvanized Undershelf, 48"Wx24"D, Mfg Part#: KRA-4824 (collectively, the Equipment).

I used this background section primarily to describe the subject matter of the contract, which is the kitchen equipment, and create a short-hand reference for the Equipment. What is most important in this section is that the description is accurate and complete. Later in the agreement I will have a covenant stating something like: "Supply Corp. will lease the Equipment to Food Service Corp. for $_____." If the definition is not accurate and complete, that covenant will not work, and neither will any of the other covenants and provisions involving the Equipment.

I was also very specific when I described the Equipment. If I had said the Equipment consisted of "an oven, a fryer, a freezer and three (3) worktables," the description would have been ambiguous. So, another way to achieve clarity is by being specific when you describe something, especially something important like the subject matter of the contract.

D. USE SHORT-HAND REFERENCES (DEFINITIONS)

After the background section you may also want to include a section listing all the defined terms in the agreement. The phrase "defined terms" is a misnomer. What we are really talking about is short-hand references; but they are commonly referred to as definitions. To this point, I have been defining terms within each sentence as they came up. Doing it that way, the convention is to describe the item in detail then put a short-hand reference in parenthesis, capitalizing the first letter of each word (you can also put quotation marks before and after the reference, but it is not necessary to do that). So, if you had a statement describing a car in a purchase and sale contract, it might look like this:

> The subject matter of this Agreement is the Tour de France-winning 1963 Ferrari 250 GTO, with the chassis number 4153 GT (the Car).

Again, you could put the definition in quotes, like this: (the "Car"). Either way is fine; just be consistent. But don't put the definition before the description, put it after. So, in the example above, don't say "the subject matter of this Agreement (the Car) is the 1963 Ferrari 250 GTO that won the Tour de France, with chassis number 4153 GT." Put the definition (the Car) at the end of the description.

The reason for doing this is to be absolutely clear you are referring to the most expensive car ever sold: The Tour de France-winning 1963 Ferrari 250 GTO, with the chassis number 4153 GT, whenever you refer to the Car in the agreement. You don't want to have to repeat all that information every time you refer to the Car, but you still want to make sure your references to it are clear, accurate, and complete. And the definition accomplishes that result.

When you are drafting definitions, avoid including rights, obligations and prohibitions in your definitions. They should all just be descriptive statements. And avoid unnecessary definitions. For example, it is appropriate to define something like this:

This Contract concerns the sale by the Company of five hundred (500) assorted holiday cards, printed in color with corresponding envelopes (the Greeting Cards).

But it is unnecessary and inappropriate to define something like this:

The Company is in the business of selling greeting cards (Greeting Cards).

If you have multiple terms in an agreement, it is sometimes better to put all the definitions in one place, usually at the beginning of the agreement, right after the background section. The convention is to alphabetize the list of terms, put each term in quotes instead of parenthesis, capitalize the first letter, use the word "means," and then state a detailed description. Here is an example from a loan agreement:

II. Definitions of Terms

The following terms have the following meanings:
"Loan" means the loan of $100,000.00 to the Borrower by the Lender pursuant to this Agreement.
"Loan Documents" means i) the Note; (ii) the Mortgage; and (iii) this Agreement.
"Mortgage" means the Mortgage of even date from the Borrower to the Lender granting the Lender a mortgage on the Mortgaged Property.
"Mortgaged Property" means the land, together with all the buildings and improvements on the land, situated at 123 Main Street in Gainesville, Florida.
"Note" means the Promissory Note of even date made by the Borrower in the amount of One Hundred Thousand Dollars ($100,000.00), payable to the order of the Lender.

I didn't define the terms Lender, Borrower, or Agreement in the list because those terms would have already been defined in the exordium. Also, there is more than one format for doing a definitions section. Another option is to do the section as two columns (one for the terms and one for the definitions) or a table, like this:

II. Definitions of Terms

Each reference in this Agreement to the following terms has the following meanings:

Loan	The loan of $100,000.00 to the Borrower by the Lender pursuant to this Agreement, to be used by Borrower for costs incurred constructing the Building.
Loan Documents	The Note, the Mortgage; this Agreement; and all other documents evidencing or securing the indebtedness evidenced by the Note.
Mortgage	The Mortgage of even date from the Borrower to the Lender granting the Lender a mortgage on the Mortgaged Property.
Mortgaged Property	The land, together with all the buildings and improvements on the land, situated at 123 Main Street in Gainesville, Florida.
Note	The Promissory Note of even date made by the Borrower in the amount of One Hundred Thousand Dollars ($100,000.00), payable to the order of the Lender.
Loan	The loan of $100,000.00 to the Borrower by the Lender pursuant to this Agreement, to be used by Borrower for costs incurred constructing the Building.

The important thing is that the presentation is clear, accurate, and complete. If the actual loan amount is $1,000,000 not $100,000 then it doesn't matter what form is used. The document has a problem. If there is a security agreement in addition to the mortgage, then the definition of the Loan Documents, and all the references to it in the agreement, will not accomplish their intended purpose. The same thing is true if there is a typo in the property address. It is important to learn the forms that are typically used for drafting contracts, but not at the expense of substance. Ultimately, it is the substance that matters most.

E. LIST REPRESENTATIONS AND WARRANTIES, IF APPLICABLE

After the definitions section, if there is one, you will on occasion want to include one more section; and that is a statement of the representations and warranties a party relied on in entering into the contract. Like definitions, representations and warranties can just be included within each provision as they come up. For example, in the background section of the employment agreement mentioned earlier, you might add a representation, like this:

> * * *
>
> C. The Employee responded to the advertisement by submitting a current resume listing his education, employment, and outside affiliations (Resume), a true and accurate copy of which is attached to this Agreement as Exhibit A.
>
> D. The Employee represents and warrants to the Employer that the information in the Resume is truthful and accurate.

If you have multiple representations and warranties you want to include in an agreement, it is usually better to put them all in one place, right after the background and definitions sections. Just make it clear who is making the representations and to whom they are being made. And since these are descriptive statements, use present or past tense. Here is an example from a purchase and sale agreement:

> **III. Representations and Warranties of Seller**
>
> The Seller makes the following representations and warranties to the Buyer:
>
> 1. The Seller arranged for the pumping of the septic on the Property once per year for every year the Seller has owned the Property.
> 2. The water from the well on the Property is potable.
> 3. The Seller obtained a permit for all improvements done to the Property.
> 4. The Seller did not store or dispose of any hazardous wastes on the Property.

As you can see, I started each of these sections with a heading describing the content. When you change to a new topic, you should add a heading before you start. And when you draft the heading, consider the same issues discussed at the beginning of this chapter on titles. Try to avoid one-word headings, like "Payment." Ask yourself "who," "what," "when," "where," or "how," depending upon which applies. So, in this case, ask, payment for what? And use the heading "Payment for Rent." Instead of "Restrictions," use "Restrictions on Use." Instead of "Termination," use "Termination of Services."

Also, if you have multiple subsections under the heading, number them (or use letters). As long as the subsections are not just an itemized list, add headings to the subsections as well. Headings are like pepperoni slices on pizza; there is no such thing as too many. The only exception is if you just have one subsection. In that case, don't number or letter it, or give it a separate heading. Only add headings to subsections if you have two or more subsections.

You will also notice I broke the text up instead of grouping it all into one paragraph. This section is short enough that either way would have probably been fine. On the one hand, you shouldn't feel like every sentence in an agreement has to be in a separate section. Grouping like provisions is a good practice to get into. On the other hand, if your section is getting bigger than about half a page, it is probably time to break it up.

To recap, a contract typically starts out with a title and an exordium. To complete the exordium, you will need the name, address, and state of organization of the parties. Next is a background section, which you can use to describe the events leading up to the contract, or the parties and the subject matter. If it is a sale of goods contract, describe the goods involved. If it is a services contract, describe the services.

A short agreement will not need a definitions section, but a lengthy document containing a lot of defined terms may need one. Representations and warranties can also be included in the background section or in the body of the agreement if there are only a few of them. But in a longer, more complex document, involving a long list of representations, the better practice is to include a representations and warranties section. Those are the sections you will typically find in the beginning of contracts.

Chapter Five
Organizing Core Covenants and Other Deal Provisions

Now that we have gone through title, exordium, background, definitions and representations, and warranties sections, we can finally get into the meat of the agreement: the core covenant and duration, if applicable. Then the details of the deal, organized by substance or chronologically, whichever is clearer.

A. Start with the Core of the Agreement

Agreements typically consist of an exchange of bilateral promises. For an agreement to work, the drafter needs to obligate both sides to do what they agreed to do. Usually, the best practice is to start broad and then get more specific. That means the agreement should start with a core covenant: a statement of the basic exchange between the parties.

I will go over three types of agreements; each involves a different core exchange. The first type is a term agreement that governs the relationship of the parties over time. An example of that is an apartment lease or employment agreement. An agreement like that will need a statement of duration or term in addition to the core covenant. The second type is a purchase and sale agreement, like a real estate purchase and sale agreement, or an agreement for the purchase of a business or equipment. A purchase and sale agreement will usually describe a due diligence period, and then a closing when the real estate or goods is exchanged for the purchase price. And the third type of agreement is one that is performed when it is signed, like a mortgage, an assignment of leases and rents, or a software license agreement. I'll give you examples of all three types of core provisions.

A core covenant for a lease might look like this:

IV. Lease of Property

The Landlord will lease the Property to the Tenant; and the Tenant will lease the Property from the Landlord.

Or this:

IV. Lease of Property

The Landlord will lease the Property to the Tenant; and the Tenant will pay the Landlord rent as provided in this Agreement.

The first example obligates the tenant to lease the property but doesn't mention rent, while the second example does. If you do it the first way, you will have an additional covenant obligating the tenant to pay rent. After both versions you will want to subsequently state things like what the rent amount is, when it is due, and how it is to be paid. You can put some of those details into the core covenant, as long as it doesn't get unwieldy. But again, the idea is to state the basic exchange first, and then get into the details later.

Here is an example of a core covenant for a purchase and sale agreement, which is an agreement that involves a transaction or exchange after a due diligence period:

IV. Sale of Condominium

The Seller will sell the Property to the Buyer; and the Buyer will buy the Property from the Seller for the Purchase Price on the Closing Date.

I was able to draft this covenant very concisely because I used a few defined terms. As long as the definitions are also accurate and clear, the covenant should work to bind both sides to do what they agreed to do.

And here is one more example. This one is from a mortgage and security agreement, which is an example of a self-executing agreement. In that type of agreement, there usually is no core exchange of covenants. Rather, the core of the agreement is simply a grant of rights, like this:

IV. Grant of Mortgage

The Borrower mortgages, grants, and conveys the Property to the Lender as security for the Loan.

I didn't use the word "will" here because this is not a covenant. The Borrower is not going to mortgage the Property sometime in the future. The mortgage is granted when the agreement is signed. The core of a self-executing agreement is actually a descriptive statement, describing what the party is doing (e.g., transferring ownership, granting rights, releasing liability).

B. DESCRIBE THE DURATION OR TERM, IF APPLICABLE

If you are drafting a term agreement, you will have to describe the term (how long the relationship will last). Also, since the term may not start right when the contract is signed, it is advisable to state the beginning and ending dates. Here is an example of a duration provision in an agreement:

V. Duration of Rental

The rental period is for three (3) years, beginning on September 1, 2020 and ending on August 30, 2020 (the Term).

If the term renews, then you would add a statement to that effect, like "the Term renews automatically unless either party sends the other party a notice of non-renewal at least thirty (30) days before the end of the Term."

C. THEN DRAFT THE SPECIFICS OF THE DEAL

Once you have drafted a good core covenant, and a duration provision, if applicable, spell out in detail the specific terms of the deal with a series of additional provisions. Obviously, the sections of the agreement will differ depending on whether the agreement is for a purchase and sale, like an agreement to buy real estate, or a relationship over time, like a lease, or if the agreement is self-executing, like a mortgage.

(1) Purchase and Sale Agreement

If the document is a contract for the purchase and sale of a condominium, for example, the seller would be required to produce the condo docs, provide the buyer with a title insurance commitment, and draft a settlement statement before the closing date. As a result, a series of supplemental covenants, might look like this:

V. Organizational Documents for Condominium

On or before the seventh (7th) day after this Agreement is signed, the Seller will provide the Buyer with the condominium documents for the Property, including the master deed, declaration of trust, and bylaws.

IV. Insurance Policy for Title

No later than fourteen (14) days before the Closing Date, the Seller will provide the Buyer with a title insurance commitment issued by a Florida licensed title insurer, with legible copies of instruments listed as exceptions.

VI. Statement of Closing Costs

At least twenty-four (24) hours before the Closing Date, the Seller will provide the Buyer with a completed Settlement Statement for the closing, detailing all costs and charges to be incurred by the Buyer and the Seller in connection with the sale of the Property.

Similarly, the buyer would be obligated to apply for financing for the purchase, have the right to inspect the property, and have the right to a final "walk through" before the closing occurs. As a result, a series of additional supplemental covenants might look like this:

VII. Inspection of Property

On or before the fifteenth (15th) day after this Agreement is signed, the Buyer may inspect the Property. If the Buyer determines that the Property is not acceptable to the Buyer, the Buyer may terminate this Agreement by delivering written notice of such termination to the Seller prior to the expiration of this inspection period.

VIII. Application for Financing

On or before the thirtieth (30th) day after this Agreement is signed, the Buyer will apply for financing for the purchase of the Property, and use diligent efforts to obtain approval for such financing, in the amount of no more than $______ at an initial interest rate of no less than %______ for a term of no more than _______ years. If the Buyer is unable to obtain such approval after the exercise of diligent effort, then the Buyer may terminate this Agreement by delivering written notice of such termination to the Seller prior to the expiration of this financing period.

IX. Walk Through Before Closing

On the day prior to the Closing Date, the Buyer may perform a walk-through inspection of the Property to confirm all items of personal property purchased by the Buyer have remained on the Property and Seller has maintained the Property as required in this Agreement.

(2) Term Agreement

If the agreement is for a relationship over time, like an equipment lease, then the core covenant might be followed by provisions relating to shipment, use, maintenance, and access, like this:

I. Shipment of Equipment

The Retailer will arrange for the shipment of the Landscaping Equipment to the Office Complex on the first day of the Term, and the shipment of the Landscaping Equipment back to the Retailer on the last day of the Term.

II. Use of Equipment

The Office Complex will use the Equipment in a safe and appropriate manner at all times. The Office Complex may permit its employees to use the Landscaping Equipment, if the employees have received appropriate training.

III. Maintenance of Equipment

The Office Complex will perform routine maintenance of the Landscaping Equipment, in accordance with the owner's manual for each piece of the Landscaping Equipment, during the Term of this Agreement.

IV. Access to Equipment

The Retailer may inspect the Landscaping Equipment at the Office Complex any time from 8:00 a.m. through 5:00 p.m., Monday through Friday.

(3) Self-Executing Agreement

If the agreement is self-executing, like a mortgage, then the core grant of rights may then lead to requirements for the payment of indebtedness and taxes, maintaining the property and repairing damage, and complying with leases, like this:

1.1 Compliance with Loan Documents

The Borrower will perform and observe all of the terms and conditions of the Loan Documents, including the obligation to make any payments as required in the Loan Documents.

1.2 Payment of Taxes

The Borrower will pay or cause to be paid all taxes, water, sewer and other utility charges, and all other charges or assessments relating to the Property or the materials stored on or in the Property and other charges and encumbrances which are or may become a lien on the Property, prior to the time when interest or penalties would accrue on such amounts.

1.3 Maintenance of Property

The Borrower will keep the Property in good order, repair and condition, reasonable wear and tear excepted, and will not permit, commit or suffer any waste, impairment, deterioration or environmental contamination of the Property.

1.4 Repair of Damage

The Borrower will promptly repair, restore, rebuild, replace, or alter as necessary any portion of the Property which may be damaged or destroyed by fire or other casualty, as nearly as possible to the condition such improvements were in prior to such damage or destruction. The Borrower will give the Lender notice of any damage to the Property no later than five (5) business days after any such damage occurs.

1.5 Compliance with Leases

The Borrower will comply with and observe its obligations as landlord under leases affecting the Property.

Depending upon the circumstances, it may be best to organize the supplemental provisions of the contract by substance. For example, you may organize an agreement with all the payment provisions in one section, and additional rights and obligations with respect to the services in another section.

But there may also be situations where it works best to organize provisions chronologically. For example, in the condominium purchase and sale agreement mentioned earlier, the seller produces the condominium documents first, and then the buyer inspects the property. After that, the buyer applies for financing. If it is approved, the seller generates a settlement statement and the Buyer does a final walkthrough, and then the final closing is held.

Start with a general statement of the core exchange and then fill in the details as you work your way through the document. If a chronological organization makes sense, then organize the supplemental provisions chronologically. If something else works better, do something else. Clarity is the goal so whatever expresses the specifics of the deal in the clearest way is the structure you should use.

Chapter Six
Organizing a Contract's Ending Sections

The ending sections of a contract usually deal with the end of the relationship. If the contract has a term, you should think about whether it is appropriate to include a termination provision or a cancellation provision. If the contract involves a closing, you will want to describe the logistics for making that happen. A list of administrative provisions (a/k/a "boilerplate") is usually included next, then a final concluding statement (a "testimonium") and signature blocks.

A. If the Contract Is a Term Agreement, Draft Provisions for Ending It Early

If the contract has a term or duration, then you will likely want to draft provisions for ending the relationship voluntarily by either cancelling or terminating it. Many attorneys use those terms interchangeably but there is a distinction between the two you should be aware of in the Uniform Commercial Code. Here is the relevant provision in the Florida version of the Code:

> * * *
>
> (3) "Termination" occurs when either party pursuant to a power created by agreement or law puts an end to the contract otherwise than for its breach. On termination, all obligations which are still executory on both sides are discharged but any right based on prior breach or performance survives.
>
> (4) "Cancellation" occurs when either party puts an end to the contract for breach by the other and its effect is the same as that of "termination" except that the canceling party also retains any remedy for breach of the whole contract or any unperformed balance.
>
> Fla. Stat. § 672.106.

Cancellation is ending the contract because the other party breached; termination is ending the contract for any other reason. Both cancellation and termination are grants of rights. So, if you were giving the landlord the right to cancel, you would do it like this:

V. Cancellation by Landlord

If the Tenant breaches any of the provisions of the Lease, the Landlord may cancel.

Like any other provision, you want to make sure it is complete. In this case, what is missing is how the Landlord would go about cancelling the Lease.

V. Cancellation by Landlord

If the Tenant breaches any of the provisions of the Lease, the Landlord may cancel by giving the Tenant written notice.

Termination is similar. If you wanted to give the tenant the right to terminate, you might draft something like this:

VI. Termination by Tenant

The Tenant may terminate the Lease for any reason.

But again, you would need to say how termination is accomplished. And since termination can happen at any time for any reason, you would likely want to add a time deadline.

VI. Termination by Tenant

The Tenant may terminate the Lease for any reason by giving written notice to the Landlord no later than thirty (30) days before the proposed termination date.

B. IF A SECURITY DEPOSIT WAS REQUIRED, PROVIDE FOR ITS RETURN

In a term agreement, like an apartment rental agreement or an equipment lease agreement, there may be a security deposit involved. If there is, then in addition to ending the relationship, the contract will also have to deal with the ultimate disposition of deposited funds. For a security deposit, you will at least need a covenant requiring the tenant to pay the deposit at the beginning of the agreement, then a provision at the end giving the landlord the right to deduct amounts for damages, and then requiring the landlord to return the balance, like this:

VI. Disposition of Security Deposit

The Landlord may deduct from the Security Deposit costs and expenses incurred by the Landlord to repair damage to the Unit caused by the Tenant during the Term. The Landlord will send the Tenant the balance of the Security Deposit no later than thirty (30) days after the end of the Term.

C. IF THE CONTRACT IS A PURCHASE AND SALE AGREEMENT, DRAFT PROVISIONS FOR CLOSING LOGISTICS

If you are drafting an agreement for a purchase of real estate or goods, you will need to describe the time and place of closing, as well as all the things each party is required to bring to the closing for the transaction to happen. Those things are sometimes called "closing deliveries." Here is a short example:

V. Closing of Sale

A. The closing is to occur at 10:00 a.m. at the offices of Dewey, Cheatham, and Howe, 999 Court Street, Alachua, Florida (the "Closing").
B. At the Closing, the Seller will execute and deliver to the Buyer a quitclaim deed for the Property.
C. At the Closing, the Buyer will deliver to the Seller, by wire transfer to the Seller's account, $125,000.00 in immediately available funds.

D. IF THE CONTRACT HAS A LIQUIDATED DAMAGES DEPOSIT, PROVIDE FOR ITS DISPOSITION.

An agreement for a sale often involves a deposit which serves as liquidated damages for one of the parties if the other fails to complete the transaction. If it does, the agreement should also provide for the ultimate disposition of the deposit if the transaction falls through. For example, a purchase and sale agreement for real estate will often provide as follows:

> **VI. Retention of Deposit**
>
> If the Buyer fails to fulfill the Buyer's obligations in this Agreement, the Seller may retain all deposits made by the Buyer under this Agreement as liquidated damages.

E. IF THE CONTRACT IS A SELF-EXECUTING AGREEMENT, THERE MAY BE NOTHING TO DO

A self-executing agreement is performed when it is signed, so there may be no need to provide for the end of the relationship. Still, something like a mortgage might have a provision obligating the mortgagee to execute and record a discharge when the underlying loan is paid. Also, it is possible for a self-executing agreement to have a term. For example, a software license agreement could be for a limited period of time. If that were the case, you would consider adding termination and/or cancellation provisions, if appropriate. Otherwise, you may not have to deal with how the relationship ends.

F. END WITH DESCRIPTIONS OF ADMINISTRATIVE POLICIES

The administrative policy statements that are often included at the end of all types of agreements are often called "boilerplate"[10] provisions. It is unfortunate

10 A boiler plate is a steel plate used in the construction of a steam boiler. Apparently, it looks similar to the typesetting plates that were used to print paper. A typesetting plate full of sections that were used over and over again became known as a "boiler plate." We don't use typesetting machines

they have that nickname because it understates their importance. Administrative provisions can have a dramatic effect on the rights and obligations of the parties. The most basic of these are merger, modification, choice of law, and choice of forum or venue.

A "merger" provision is a description of the parole evidence rule. Do you remember the rule from contracts class? If a contract is complete and final, prior statements are merged into the document and cannot be used to contradict its terms. A merger provision is a statement of that principle; it is a descriptive statement, not an obligation, grant of rights, or prohibition. Here is an example:

XIII. Integration of Agreement

This Agreement is the complete and final agreement between the parties regarding the sale of the Business. All prior statements, understandings, and agreements are merged into this Agreement.

I think of a "modification" provision as the corollary to a merger provision. A merger provision deals with statements and agreements made before the contract is signed. A modification provision deals with agreements made after the contract is signed. A modification is not a grant of rights; the parties already have the right to modify the contract. It could be drafted as a condition to an obligation. "If the parties want to modify, they will only modify in writing." Or, it could be a prohibition. "The parties will not modify orally." But drafting it that way does not really accomplish the desired effect. You don't want to sue the other party for breach; you want the modification to be invalid. For that reason, I would do the provision as another policy statement, like this:

XIV. Modification of Agreement

Any amendment of this Agreement is invalid unless it is in writing, signed by both parties, and states the nature of the modification, and the provision to which it applies.

anymore, but many attorneys still refer to language that is used over and over again without modification, like the administrative provisions at the end of contracts, as "boiler plate."

Choice of law is another provision that can only be done as a descriptive statement. It is not an obligation; you can't obligate the judge to apply a specific state's law. And it is not a grant of rights or a prohibition. Often a choice of law provision is drafted just to make clear what law applies to breach of contract claims. But it can be drafted more broadly to include tort and statutory claims arising out of whatever subject matter the contract deals with. And it can be drafted to include conflicts of law principles, assuming the law of the forum state allows for the parties to choose what state's conflicts of law principles apply to the interpretation of the provision. Here is an example that incorporates all three of those issues:

XV. Choice of Law

Florida law governs the interpretation of this Agreement, including tort and statutory claims arising out of the provision of the Services. Florida conflicts of law principles govern the interpretation of this provision.

As for choice of forum, it wouldn't make sense to draft it as a grant of rights (the parties already have the right to sue in the applicable forum). It could be drafted as a condition to an obligation. "If either party sues, they will do so only in the chosen forum." Or a prohibition: "if either party sues, they will not do so in any forum other than the chosen forum." But again, you don't want to sue the party for breach if they bring an action in the wrong forum. You are describing a choice the parties have made, and you want the court to respect that choice. So, I would recommend drafting a choice of forum provision as a statement of policy too. Also, remember to make clear that the forum is mandatory and exclusive, and applicable only to litigation, like this:

XVI. Choice of Forum

The mandatory and exclusive venue for any litigation arising out of this Agreement lies in Jefferson County, Florida.

________ ________

I put the language in bold and included initial lines to help bolster the enforceability of the provision, since it potentially affects the constitutional due process rights of the parties. If you add initial lines, make sure the signers actually initial above the lines. If they don't, adding them may have the opposite of the intended effect.

There are multiple additional administrative provisions in contracts, and I would draft them all in a similar fashion. Here are some more examples:

10. Severability of Agreement

This Agreement is severable. If any provision is unenforceable, that provision is severed, and the remaining provisions continue in effect.

11. Non-Assignability of Agreement

This Agreement is not assignable. Any purported assignment of this Agreement by either party is invalid.

12. Binding Nature of Agreement

This Agreement inures to the benefit of and is binding on all permitted successors and assigns.

13. Headings of Agreement

The headings in this Agreement are for reference purposes only and are not intended to affect the meaning or interpretation of this Agreement in any way.

14. Counterparts of Agreement

If the parties execute this Agreement in one or more counterparts, then all of such counterparts constitute only one Agreement.

15. Cumulative Nature of Remedies

All rights and remedies provided in this Agreement are cumulative and not exclusive of any other rights or remedies that are to be available to the parties.

G. DRAFT A TESTIMONIUM (CLOSING STATEMENT) BEFORE THE SIGNATURE BLOCKS

After the administrative provisions of a contract comes something called the "testimonium."[11] In the old days, the testimonium would contain lots of legalese. For example, one style was to end the contract with a statement like this: "Witness our hands and seals this __ day of _____, 20__." Today we leave the legalese out and just recite in plain English that the parties are signing as of the date in the exordium. That way the document doesn't have multiple different dates, and it is clear what the correct date is. Here is a sample testimonium:

> Executed by the parties as of the date above.

H. DRAFT APPROPRIATE SIGNATURE BLOCKS FOR EACH PARTY

After the testimonium there is just one more thing needed to make the contract complete and that is a set of signature blocks, one for each party. What is most important when doing the signature blocks is distinguishing between a person who is signing as an individual and a person who is signing on behalf of an entity. If the former, the person will be personally liable for damages resulting from any contract breach. If the latter, the entity, not the person, will bear that liability.

Here is an example of a signature block for an individual:

> ______________________________
>
> [Name of Signer]

And here is an example of a signature block for an entity (a corporation):

11 Testimonium is Latin for "witness" or "attestation." Lewis & Short, *Latin Dictionary.*

____

[Name of Corporation]
By: [Name of Signer] [Title]

If the party is an entity containing another entity, like a limited partnership with a corporation as its general partner, you would do the signature block like this:

Realty Associates L.P.,
By its General Partner,

____

[Name of Corporation]
By: [Name of Signer] [Title]

To finish a contract, think about how the relationship will end and whether any funds need to be accounted for, including any money held on deposit. Then draft appropriate policy provisions. Most of the time they should be done as descriptive statements. Add a testimonium but leave out the legalese. And draft appropriate signature blocks, depending upon whether each party is a person or an entity.

Those are the basic elements of a contract.[12] Now that you have learned the basics of how to draft and organize contract provisions, you should be able to draft a simple contract. You may be at a closing and the parties may need someone to draft an escrow agreement right then and there. You may also be a litigator handling a case that settles on the courthouse steps, and you may have to draft the settlement agreement before everyone goes home. In either case, you should be able to draft a simple contract based on what you've learned so far.

12 I also included a "Contract Drafting Checklist" at the end of this handbook. The checklist covers both the basics of how to draft and organize contract provisions.

Practice Exercises

1. Draft an exordium for a software license agreement to be signed today. The parties are Vision Software, LLC and John Rodriguez. Vision is organized under Florida law. Both parties are located in Miami. Vision is at 123 Main Street; and John lives at 76 Palm Court.
2. Draft a core covenant for a lease of kitchen equipment by a corporation to a cook.
3. Draft a signature block for Tropical Apartments L.P. The limited partners are Mary and Lena Vasquez. The general partner is Casa Vasquez, Ltd. The president of Casa Vasquez is Sam Vasquez.
4. Draft a definition for a car in the background section of an agreement (the car is the subject matter of the agreement). The car will be a four-door hybrid. It will be painted white. And, it will have tinted windows.
5. Draft a simple contract based on the Transcript for Laptop Purchase Agreement in the appendix to this Handbook.

Answers to Practice Exercises

1. On ________ ___, 20___, Vision Software LLC, a Florida limited liability company, having an office at 123 Main Street, Miami, Florida and John Rodriguez, an individual having a residence at 76 Palm Court, Miami, Florida enter into this software license agreement. The parties mutually agree as follows:
2. The corporation will lease the kitchen equipment to the cook; and the cook will pay the corporation for the use of the equipment.

   Or

   The corporation will lease the kitchen equipment to the cook; and the cook will lease the kitchen equipment from the corporation.
3. Tropical Apartments l.P.,

   By its General Partner,

   ____

   Casa Vasquez, Ltd.

   By: Sam Vasquez, President
4. The subject matter of this Agreement is a four-door hybrid car, painted white, with tinted windows (Car).

   Or

   This Agreement concerns a car having the following features: four doors, hybrid, white, tinted windows (the Car).
5. See the Sample Laptop Purchase Agreement in the appendix at the end of this Handbook.

Chapter Seven
Brainstorming

There is more to drafting contracts than transcribing what the client tells you and writing it in a clear and organized way. Part of the lawyer's job is to document whatever the client says the deal is. But part of the lawyer's job is also to think into the future about all the different things that could happen after the agreement is signed; and make sure the client's interests are protected should any of those contingencies occur. I call all that "brainstorming." The client tells you what the agreement is, and then you try to think of what additional issues should be addressed, and what provisions you might add to better protect the client or advance the client's interests.

A. Addressing Possible Contingencies

Suppose the seller agrees to sell a commercial building to the buyer and hires you to draft a purchase and sale agreement. Likely the parties talked about the features of the building, the price and what would have to happen for the closing to occur. They may have even put together a timeline and scheduled a date for completion. But they probably did not talk about what would happen if the building burned to the ground before the closing took place. That's the type of thing the lawyer needs to think about and address in the agreement in addition to everything else.

As another example, suppose two partners agree to start a law firm together and hire you to draft a partnership agreement. They probably talked about what their practice would consist of, where their office would be, and how they would share profits and divide expenses. But they probably didn't discuss what would happen if at some time in the future one of them died or decided to leave the partnership. Again, that is an issue the lawyer will have to raise, resolve between the parties, and then make part of the agreement. Once you know the terms of the deal, brainstorm for issues that were left out and contingencies that may happen in the future. Then follow up with the client, resolve the issues and add the additional language to the agreement.

There are some contingencies that you will likely want to address in virtually every contract you draft. For example, if you represent a provider of goods or services, how can you protect the client from the possibility the client will have trouble getting paid at some point in the future? What if you are on the other side, representing a client who may, for innocent reasons, be late making a payment after the agreement is signed? What can you do to help both parties to avoid the cost and expense of any future litigation? What if the client gets sued by the other side or some third party? What can you do to limit the client's exposure to liability? Because these issues are so common, you should be aware of how they are typically addressed.

1) Giving Payment Provisions "Teeth"

Most contracts involve an exchange of good or services for money. As a result, there is usually a risk that, if you represent the payee, your client will have difficulty getting the other side to pay on time. What can you do then to make the payment provisions in the agreement more effective?

One thing you can do is impose a late fee if payments are late:

> A. On or before _______ ___, 20___, the Buyer will pay the Seller $____.
> B. If the Buyer pays late, the Buyer will also pay the Seller a late fee of $____.

If that's not enough, have the fee accrue with time, so the later the payment, the bigger the fee.

> A. On or before _______ ___, 20___, the Buyer will pay the Seller $____.
> B. If the Buyer pays late, the Buyer will also pay the Seller a late fee of $____of the payment amount for every day that the payment is late.

Another thing you can do is make it clear timeliness is material to the agreement, so that lateness is a material breach. Just be aware that provision will work both ways. The other side has to perform on time, but your client has to perform on time too:

16. Time of Essence

Time is of the essence with respect to all of the obligations in this Agreement.

You can also add that if it is necessary to sue to collect amounts unpaid, the losing party will pay the costs of doing so. But, again, unless you draft the language to apply only to just the other party, which the other party is unlikely to agree to, this type of provision also works both ways.

17. Costs of Collection

The losing party will pay all reasonable attorneys' fees and costs incurred by the prevailing party in enforcing this Agreement.

You should always be thinking not just about the form, but also about the substance of what you are drafting. You need to make sure what you are doing accurately represents the terms the parties agreed to. But you should also be trying to think of ways to better protect your clients' interests. You should always be looking for opportunities to add value to the deal.

2) Avoiding Disputes Between the Parties

If you are on the other side of the transaction, and you represent the person making the payments, you should consider the possibility that your client may – for reasons that are not the client's fault – find himself or herself in breach of the agreement. If that occurs, what can you do to help the client avoid getting sued? What can you do to give the client the opportunity to fix the situation, so that the contract is not cancelled, and the relationship can continue?

One thing you could do is add a grace period to the payment provisions. To do that, you leave the due date the same, but change the late fee so that it doesn't start until the end of the grace period, like this:

A. On or before ________ ___, 20___, the Buyer will pay the Seller $____.
B. If the Buyer pays more than five (5) days late, the Buyer will also pay the Seller a late fee of $____.

Another way to avoid litigation is for one party to give the other party notice of default and an opportunity to cure before commencing litigation. In a loan agreement, that is typically done by giving the lender the right to exercise those of its rights and remedies as it deems appropriate only after an "Event of Default." A breach of an agreement provision is not enough. An "Event of Default" occurs after the borrower is given notice of the default and a period of time within which to cure the default. If the borrower fails to cure within the prescribed period, then there is an "Event of Default," and the lender has the right to take action, including "accelerating" the loan. In other words, the lender has the right to declare the entire balance due and payable now instead of payable over time. Here are excerpts from two applicable provisions in a loan agreement:

SECTION 7. EVENTS OF DEFAULT

The occurrence of any one or more of the following events constitutes an "Event of Default" under the terms of this Agreement:

* * *

7.3 The Borrower fails to pay the principal of, or fees, or interest on, the Note or any other indebtedness of the Borrower under the Loan Documents after the same is due and payable and such failure continues beyond the date which is ten (10) days after written demand is made by the Lender.

7.4 The Borrower defaults in the due observance or performance of any other covenant, condition, or agreement to be observed or performed by the Borrower pursuant to the terms of any of the Loan Documents and such default remains uncured thirty (30) days after written notice is given by the Lender to the Borrower.

SECTION 8. RIGHTS ON DEFAULT

Upon the occurrence of any one or more of the Events of Default enumerated in the foregoing Section 7, and at any time thereafter, then:

8.1 The Lender may declare all indebtedness due under the Note and any and all other indebtedness of the Borrower to the Lender due under the other Loan Documents or otherwise to be due and payable, whether or not the indebtedness evidenced by the Note or the other Loan Documents is otherwise due and payable and whether or not the Lender has initiated any foreclosure or other action for the enforcement pursuant to the provisions of the Loan Documents, whereupon all indebtedness due under the Note and the other Loan Documents and any other such indebtedness becomes immediately due and payable, both as to principal and interest, without presentment, demand, protest, or notice of any kind, all of which are expressly waived by the Borrower.

3) Handling Disputes Outside of Litigation

Often it is in the interests of both parties to resolve any disputes without resorting to litigation. This is particularly true for disputes over a relatively small amount, like the amount of deposits routinely collected in connection with residential purchase and sale contracts and residential leases. What can you do in a situation like that to help the parties avoid litigation?

This issue is most commonly addressed by having the parties agree up front to resolve any disputes through mediation or arbitration. Here is an example of a covenant to mediate disputes:

16. Mediation of Disputes

Before resorting to litigation, the Buyer and Seller will attempt to settle any disputes arising out of this Agreement in an amicable manner through mediation with a Florida certified or court appointed mediator pursuant to Florida Rules for Certified and Court-Appointed Mediators.

If the client wants the mechanism to be binding on the parties, and the client's concern with avoiding disputes is not so much with the cost of litigation but rather with the technical nature of the contract and likely unfamiliarity of any civil judge or jury with the issues dealt with in the contract, arbitration may be another option. Unlike mediation, arbitration is binding, and you can arbitrate a dispute with an arbitrator who has expertise in a specific area. For example, you could draft a provision requiring the parties to submit disputes to an arbitrator having expertise with technology, like this:

17. Arbitration of Disputes

The parties will submit any controversy or claim arising out of or relating to this Contract, or any breach of this Contract, to be resolved and determined by binding arbitration administered by a member of the Florida Circuit-Civil Mediator Society having case experience with technology pursuant to the Florida Arbitration Code, Fla. Stat. §§ 682.01 through 682.25.

Other issues which can also be dealt with in a mediation or arbitration clause include who will pay for the mediator or arbitrator and how that person will be selected, where and when the mediation or arbitration will take place, what law will apply, and whether attorney's fees are recoverable.

4) Limiting the Liability of a Party to the Other

If the client does get sued, how can the client limit its liability to the other side? If the contract is for the sale of goods, you can use your knowledge of the Uniform Commercial Code to better protect the client's interests. For example, the Code gives a seller the right to exclude or modify implied warranties:

*   *   *

(2) Subject to subsection (3), to exclude or modify the implied warranty of merchantability or any part of it, the language must mention merchantability and in case of a writing must be conspicuous; and, to exclude or modify any implied warranty of fitness, the exclusion must be by a writing and conspicuous. Language to exclude all implied warranties of fitness is sufficient if it states, for example, that "There are no warranties which extend beyond the description on the face hereof."

Fla. Stat. §672.316.

As you can see, the exclusion has to be conspicuous. The statute says merchantability must be mentioned, although the sample language doesn't mention merchantability. To exclude both, you might draft something like this:

18. Exclusion of Implied Warranties

THE IMPLIED WARRANTIES OF MERCHANTABILITY AND FITNESS FOR USE ARE EXCLUDED FROM THIS AGREEMENT.

The Code also gives a seller the right to limit or exclude consequential damages:

*   *   *

(3) Consequential damages may be limited or excluded unless the limitation or exclusion is unconscionable. Limitation of consequential damages for injury to the person in the case of consumer goods is prima facie unconscionable but limitation of damages where the loss is commercial is not.

Fla. Stat. §672.719.

Here is another sample provision:

18. Exclusion of Consequential Damages

Consequential damages for any breach of contract claim based on this Agreement are also excluded.

5) Protecting Against Third Party Claims

The client may also have the risk of being sued by a third party. The classic case is where the services are provided to a property owner. If someone gets hurt, the service provider will get sued, and the owner will likely be sued as well. Under these circumstances, protecting the client from liability can be achieved by making sure the client will be indemnified for any losses the client incurs (i.e. the other party to the contract will pay if the client is sued by a third party). An indemnity provision is a covenant running from the "indemnitor" to the "indemnitee." Typically, the language used is "[the indemnitor] will indemnify and hold harmless [the indemnitee] from and against________." Also, an indemnification provision should mention negligence claims and claims seeking attorney's fees, if they are included; and it should be limited to claims arising out of the applicable transaction or relationship, so that it is not overbroad. Here is a sample provision:

19. Indemnification of Claims

The Subcontractor will indemnify and hold harmless the Owner, its officers, directors, agents, and employees, from and against all third-party claims, causes of action, lawsuits and proceedings, including claims for negligence, requesting damages, including personal injuries, property damages and economic losses, and reasonable attorney's fees, arising out of the lease of the Equipment.

The client is less likely to have to pay a judgment if the person or entity providing the services has enough money to pay for the loss. As a result, it is also appropriate to make sure the other side has insurance for the types of claims that might arise from the performance of services (or any damage to property or equipment rented). Like an indemnity clause, an insurance provision is also a covenant. In addition to requiring the party to obtain insurance, it should require the party to "maintain" the insurance (i.e. not let the insurance lapse). Also, it is important to mention the type of insurance required and the policy amounts, as well as add language requiring the party to add the other side as an additional insured or loss payee and produce proof of insurance upon request, like this:

20. Insurance for Equipment

The Subcontractor will maintain insurance covering liability for personal injury in the amount of at least $_____, loss and damage to the Equipment for not less than full replacement value of the Equipment, which is $_________, and property damage insurance in the amount of at least $___________. The Subcontractor will name the Owner as a beneficiary or additional insured under the applicable policies. The Subcontractor will also provide the Owner with copies of certificates evidencing all such insurance upon request.

Those are some examples of the types of provisions you might use to protect a client from future contingencies that could hurt the client's interests. Contract drafting is not just writing. You need to think of all the things that could happen in the future, and all the ways a deal could go wrong. Then draft language that will protect your client should any of those contingencies occur. Brainstorming is where you really have the opportunity to provide valuable advice and draft an effective agreement.

Get up to speed first, then draft clear, consistent provisions and organize them in into a contract. After you do that, Brainstorm. Think into the future about all the different things that could happen after the agreement is signed; and make sure the client's interests are protected should any of those contingencies occur.

Chapter Eight
Drafting with Precedent Language and Documents

When a lawyer drafts a document from scratch in the real world, she doesn't typically do so in a vacum. Law students are prohibited from copying language drafted by someone else, but lawyers do that all the time. Your law professor is testing you on how well you can draft on your own. Your client doesn't care how you got the language you are using, as long as it works. You can't violate anyone's copyright, but otherwise you can collect well drafted provisions and documents and use them to draft whatever type of contracts you need.

There are two ways to draft with precedent language. One is to look at a variety of sample documents, take provisions from each document, and put them all together to make a single agreement. I had a client once who wanted a me to draft an option to purchase air rights to construct residences over commercial real estate in urban areas. I couldn't find a sample document that was anything close to what I needed. But I was able to draft an appropriate agreement by looking at analogous situations and using sample language from a number of different documents.

The other way to draft with precedent language is to find a sample agreement that is close to what you are trying to do, and revise it as appropriate. If you are drafting something like a promissory note or a mortgage, you should have no problem finding sample documents. Using a sample agreement will likely save you a lot of time. And you can also learn a lot about the types of provisions that are typically included in notes and mortgages by looking at precedent documents.

Lawers have always had access to thousands of sample agreements on every subject you could imagine. Law libraries are an excellent source of documents. Because of the internet, there are even more sources of sample documents available, and they are easier to access. Westlaw has a service called "Practical Law" that is a good source for sample agreements. Westlaw can be costly to use, but there are plenty of free sites on the internet. The Securities and Exchange Commission service called EDGAR (Electronic Data Gathering, Analysis, and Retrieval) is free a source that can be used to search for sample business documents. Also, there is a free website called www.onecle that is a potential source for sample agreements.

I would recommend that you stay away from pay sites like Rocketlawyer and LegalZoom. You can't give a client a document they could have obained themselves by visiting someone else's website. Because sites like that are widely available now, you also have to produce a better product than what those sites sell. No reasonable savy client is going to pay you to draft a contract if they can get something just as good by going on line.

If you work for a law firm, the firm will probably have a collection of sample documents you can use. If you are practicing on your own, you will want to save copies of the contracts you receive from other attorneys, so you can start to create your own database of samples. When you see a provision another attorney has drafted particularly well, learn from what that attorney has done to improve the language you usually use. After a while, you will have your own collection of sample documents and provisions.

When you are considering adopting language someone else drafted, it is important to determine where the language came from. Among other things, was it drafted for a client with interests like those of your client, and was it used in a transaction similar to the one you are involved in. For example, you likely wouldn't want to use form language from a lease written on behalf of a landlord in a contract you are drafting for a tenant. And it likely wouldn't be appropriate to use provisions from a residential lease to use for commercial space.

In addition, whenever you use langauge from another document, you will have to revise it to conform to the style of the document you are drafting. If the precedent language contains legalese, take it out. If the precedent uses "shall" for covenants and you use "will," change the language to make it consistent with the rest of your document. And if language you want to use refers to the landlord as "Owner," while your document uses use the term Landlord, you will need to change language you are using from the precedent document. Don't just copy what you have found. Legal documents are not generic commodities you can just download from the internet and hand to a client. Even if you are using precedent langauge or a form document, you still need to tailor it to circumtances you are involved with.

I started this book with a discussion of how to draft from scratch without using precedent language and documents because you really have to know that to use precedents well. There is nothing worse than a contract produced by an attorney that is a collection of provisions drafted in different styles for different clients in different circumstances, and has never been revised to make it uniform and appropriate for the transaction it is used in. When you see documents like that you will know the drafter has no idea what he is doing. If you do it right, there is more to drafting with precedent language and documents than just copying someone else's work.

Chapter Nine
Tailoring Form Documents for a Deal

Most of the time transactional lawyers draft by starting with a form document and then tailoring it for use in a specific deal. Clients usually don't want you to "reinvent the wheel" because of the time and expense involved in doing so. It is more efficient to start with a form. As a result, what you will likely spend most of your time doing in practice is working with complex forms that have already been drafted by someone else. So, for example, if you're working at a firm in the commercial lending department, you'll probably be working with a set of documents the firm uses for all its commercial lending transactions. You won't have to draft the documents from scratch. Instead, you'll need to tailor the forms to conform to a particular deal, and then close the deal. Also, when you are on the other side of a transaction, your job will be to revise a set of completed documents to better reflect the other side's interests. Regardless of the situation, you need to recognize working with existing forms is very different than drafting a contract from scratch. If you aren't familiar with the form, you need to study it first so you understand what it says and how it was put together. Draft the revisions the same way the rest of the document is drafted. Then read the document again to see if any other provisions are affected by the changes you made. And keep track of all the revised drafts you create.

A. Read the Form to Familiarize Yourself with the Substance and Structure

A lengthy business contract can be intimidating if you are not familiar with it. You may not know the subject matter; and the terminology may be alien to you. The type may be small and the paragraphs densely packed. Most people avoid reading contracts like that. But someone has to read them to figure out what they say. And that someone is you.

So just take your time and go through the document section by section. If there are terms you don't recognize, look them up. If the applicable law is something you are not familiar with, you may have to do a little research. Take breaks if you lose your concentration. The ability to scour a lengthy business document is a skill you will develop with time.

Depending upon the circumstances, you will likely want to take notes as you read; and it may help you to create an outline of the contract's terms. The situation is analogous to reading a long, complex statute for the first time. You really need to study the language to fully understand how the document works and how it was put together. You can't revise one section and then be oblivious to what is contained in the rest of the form. So do what you have to do to familiarize yourself with the document before you start revising it.

B. DRAFT THE REVISIONS THE SAME WAY THE DOCUMENT WAS DRAFTED

When you are ready to start filling in the blanks and making revisions, there are three rules I would recommend you follow. First, you need to draft the revisions the same way the rest of the document was drafted, even if it was drafted differently than what you learned in the first few chapters of this book. In other words, make whatever changes you have fit in with the rest of the document. If you are adding a background provision, and the form starts each background provision with the word "whereas," then you should start your background provision the same way, even though "whereas" is legalese. If the form uses "shall" for covenants, you should use "shall" for covenants, even if you agree with me that "will" is plainer English than "shall." Also, use the document's definitions in the provisions you draft.

As a practical matter, you can't revamp every document from beginning to end to conform to what you learned in this book, and then send the client a bill for the time you spent doing something you weren't asked to do. You still need to be concerned with clarity, completion, and accuracy; but you also need to follow the same rules the original drafter followed when she drafted the document. Everyone drafts a little differently; when you are working on someone else's documents, you need to respect the decisions the drafter made and the style she felt was appropriate. So, rule number one is draft the revisions the same way the document was drafted, even if it was drafted differently than what you learned so far.

C. READ CLOSELY THE REST OF THE DOCUMENT TO SEE IF OTHER PROVISIONS ARE AFFECTED

The second important thing you need to realize when you are revising a complex form is that it is not enough just to make changes here and there, and then consider the draft complete. Whenever you change any language in a complex document, you also need to read closely the rest of the provisions to see if they are affected. If they are, you need to either confirm the provisions still work as intended with the new language or you need to revise the provisions as well. The documents used in large commercial deals are often complicated; you have to appreciate that complexity and make sure your revisions don't screw up the rest of the form. Rule number two then is to closely read the rest of the document whenever you add to, delete, or change the language that is already there.

If the document is set up for a corporation, for example, and you are filling in the blanks, and it turns out the borrower is a sole proprietorship, then check to see if there are other provisions of the document that have to be changed. For example, the representation and warranty that "the Borrower is a duly organized and existing Florida corporation" will need to be revised. The covenant that "the Borrower will file annual reports with the Secretary of State" will have to be revised. And the prohibition that "the Borrower will not amend its articles of organization without the Lender's consent" will also need to be changed.

Any time you delete a defined term you will need to search through the document for every time when that term was used and (1) confirm deleting the term is appropriate (it may have been used for something you didn't anticipate); (2) delete the term; and (3) make sure the remaining language still works properly (e.g. if the only reason for the provision was to say something about the term, then you would delete the whole thing).

Also, when you delete an entire subsection in an agreement, realize that doing that will throw off the numbering of subsequent subsections. When you do that, either replace the deleted language with the statement "intentionally omitted" or renumber the entire section. Also, if you renumber the entire section, make sure references to the renumbered paragraphs elsewhere in the document are also changed. You might have a provision that says a party can exercise its rights in "paragraph seven." If you deleted a paragraph, and paragraph seven is now paragraph six, you need to change the reference to paragraph seven as well. And, of course, you also need to write and organize your provisions the same way they are drafted in the agreement.

Needless to say, it is difficult to pour through a long document over and over, every time you do a new deal, to make sure the substance matches what the client actually agreed to do, and all the factual information is correct. To make it easier, some practitioners print out the document and read it with pen in hand, rather than on a computer screen. Others read the contract slowly out loud to help them spot issues. I find it helps to look at one subject at a time, so I check all the paragraph numbering in one pass through, double check all the dates and dollar amounts in another pass through, check for name and address spelling, and then check for proper usage of defined terms. Another good habit to get into is going back to the notes of your original client conference to make sure you addressed all the issues. Complex documents tend to involve high dollar amounts. When a client entrusts you with handling a large transaction, there is really no such thing as being too careful.

D. KEEP TRACK OF ANY CHANGES YOU MAKE

Rule number three is keep track of any changes you make to a form document. Always start with a copy of the original document and keep the original even if you don't need it anymore. The changes you make for one deal may not be appropriate to use in another deal you work on in the future. If they aren't, it may make a lot more sense to go back to the original document and change that, than change the revised version again. Also, when you are working on a large transaction, you will have changes to your documents coming from a number of different sources. You need to keep track of who changed what when. Among other things, circumstances may arise where you will need to unwind some of the changes and go back to an earlier version.

Once you have a set of documents drafted, and before you send them to the other side, send a set of drafts to your client to review. Make sure the changes are highlighted and the client can see what you did, especially the factual information you entered, and confirm it is accurate. You may have misheard something the client said, or the client may have misspoken. Regardless of the reason, it is important to fix any mistakes before the documents go out the door.

Some clients will just skim what you send them, and then send it back with a thank you note (in fact some clients may think of the drafting as your job and not understand why you are seeking their input). Other clients will go through your edits with a fine-tooth comb and give you a lot of feedback. In my opinion the latter type is far preferable to work with. Just don't get defensive if you get a lot of comments. Better to incorporate those suggestions and make the agreement perfectly match what the client wants, than to go without them and have a document signed that doesn't accurately conform to the deal.

Once all the proofreading is done, provide the documents to the attorney on the other side of the transaction. In a commercial transaction, the attorney representing the other side will likely have additional proposed revisions. You will have responses to those revisions. And there may be other parties in the transaction who also want to revise the documents. As a result, it is important to keep track of all these changes, who made them, and when they were made. In the old days, that was done by keeping paper copies of each set of revisions in manila files. Today, it is more common to just keep copies of the computer files, labeled appropriately. For example, a file containing the borrower's first set of revisions to a loan agreement might have a filename like this: "loanagre.rev1.borr.2.28.2019.doc"

As for the proposed changes, they are usually done by marking up the original document. When paper was popular, an attorney would handwrite comments on a "hard copy" of the agreement and send it to the other side by "fax." Today, it is more common to use the "track changes" feature in a program like Word,[13] and then send the comments to the other side by e-mail.

If you are the original producer of the document at issue, you have an interest in making sure all the requested revisions work together, and the document is still clear and coherent after it is revised. Sometimes when there are too many "cooks in the kitchen," the revisions can get out of hand, and the document suffers. If you are the original drafter, it is part of your job not to let that happen. After all the changes are in, you may have to go back through the document to make everything hang together more uniformly, and then circulate a revised draft.

Once you have the document in final form, save it in some way that it cannot be changed. If you are handling a closing, the other parties are relying on you to produce the final version of the document at the closing. As a practical matter there isn't enough time for every attorney to proofread every page of every document while everyone else is at the closing waiting to sign. So, everyone has to rely on you. And if you let them down by unintentionally substituting the

13 You could also use comment bubbles or even footnotes.

wrong draft, your reputation will be irreparably harmed. So always keep careful track of which document is the final version!

Remember, completing a form document for a deal is not just an exercise in filling in the blanks. If it were, they wouldn't be asking you to do it. Your job is to tailor the document to the deal. That involves closely reading the document and revising it with an appreciation of its complexity and how it was originally put together. So, use your brain, and think about whether the facts fit the substantive provisions. If they don't, make appropriate revisions to the language. And make the changes fit by following the same protocols the original drafter followed. That is how you complete a set of form documents for a deal.

Practice Exercise

Complete the Construction Loan Agreement at the end of this Handbook for the following deal:

a. The borrower is an individual named Alberto Salvatori. He lives at 333 South Street in Micanopy, Florida. The lender is Archer Bank, which has a branch office in Micanopy at 4 Sunrise Terrace.
b. The project will be a single-family home in Macintosh, Florida. The address is 7 Palm Court, Macintosh. The borrower plans to occupy the property after the closing.
c. The loan is for $150,000. There will be no retainage.
d. There are no junior lenders.
e. The lender approved Homes, Inc. as the contractor for the project. There is no architect. When the project is done, the contractor will certify compliance with applicable laws.
f. The borrower will be using part of the loan to acquire the property.

Answer to Practice Exercise

See the Construction Loan Agreement for Salvatori Project at the end of this Handbook.

Chapter Ten

Revising the Other Side's Completed Documents

The other situation you will likely be involved in is proposing revisions to a completed document when you represent the other side in a deal (i.e. you are not the one who completed the form or drafted the original document).[14] That usually involves qualifying the contract language, imposing conditions, and narrowing the scope of the original provisions. If your client is asked to sign a document you didn't draft, chances are very good you will need to go through this aspect of dealing with complex documents. And that is true even if the other side claims they are using a "standard" form and presents it to you like it's written in stone.[15]

A. Qualifying the Language

The primary way you protect the client's interests in documents you have not drafted yourself is by qualifying the language in the documents. For example, suppose there is a covenant in the document that says this:

> The Manager will remove all lead paint from the interior of the Premises.

If you represent the owner of the premises, you could make that obligation stronger by changing it to this:

14 If you have the option to be the original drafter, take advantage of that opportunity. It is usually better to be the original drafter than to have to revise documents someone else drafted. However, you may not have that opportunity if, for example, you represent borrowers not lenders.

15 The one exception to this rule I am aware of is for the loan documents used by Fannie Mae. Those loans are securitized and sold in the secondary market. For that and other reasons, there is really nothing you can do to revise the language on behalf of a borrower. It is still important to explain to the borrower what the substance of those documents is. But this discussion on revising a document to protect a client's interests really doesn't apply in that context.

> The Manager will remove all lead paint from the interior of the Premises to the satisfaction of the Owner.

If the owner drafted the language and you represented the manager, you could make the language weaker by revising it to this:

> The Manager will use reasonable efforts to remove all lead paint from the interior of the Premises.

And if both parties were negotiating the language, they might agree on an objective standard that is somewhere in between those two extremes by revising it to say this:

> The Manager will remove all lead paint from the interior of the Premises in a good and workmanlike manner.

Depending on who you represent, you can qualify the language to better serve your client's interests. By qualifying the language, you are changing the level of risk that each party has to bear. The first example puts all the risk on the manager. In the second example, the owner is taking more risk.

Another example might be the language used in representations and warranties. A seller in a real estate transaction might not be comfortable representing that "there are no hazardous wastes on the Property." The seller would know whether or not the seller dumped any hazardous wastes on the property. But the seller would have no way of knowing what happened before the seller owned the property. So, to better protect the seller's interests, the representation could be modified to say, "to the best of the Seller's knowledge, there are no hazardous wastes on the Property." By making that qualification, you transfer some of the risk from the seller to the buyer.

B. IMPOSING CONDITIONS ON THE LANGUAGE

You can also change the allocation of risk in a document by imposing conditions on the language. Suppose, for example, an employer has the right to test an employee's blood for the presence of illegal drugs. The applicable provision might simply say this:

> The Employer may obtain and test a sample of the Employee's blood to look for the presence of illegal drugs; and the Employee will submit to such tests when requested.

You could limit the employer's rights by imposing conditions on the language, like this:

> After first giving the Employee written notice at least thirty (30) days before the proposed test date, the Employer may obtain and test a sample of the Employee's blood to look for the presence of illegal drugs; and the Employee will submit to such tests, unless the Employee has a valid medical reason for refusing to do so.

By imposing these conditions, you transfer some of the risk from the employee to the employer.

C. NARROWING THE SCOPE OF LANGUAGE

Yet another option is to narrow the scope of the language. This is particularly helpful when dealing with exculpatory provisions, which are often drafted in an unreasonably broad way. For example, here is a release from an apartment lease:

> The Tenant releases, remises and forever discharges the Landlord, and his employees and agents, from any claims, causes of action or lawsuits the Tenant has now or may have in the future.

Ideally, you would just delete that provision, if you represent a tenant. But at the very least you can revise it to make the language narrower, like this:

> The Tenant releases, remises and forever discharges the Landlord from any claims, causes of action or lawsuits arising out of the use of the Property the Tenant has now and is currently aware of.

When you are proposing changes like this, you should do the changes in a manner that shows the other attorney what you're proposing to revise; and makes it easy for the other attorney to accept your changes, if she is agreeable to making them. Don't just ask the attorney to revise a provision to address an issue you are concerned about. Make the revisions for her, so that she can just accept the change if she is agreeable. For example, if I were requesting a revision to the release provision above, I would do it like this:

> The Tenant releases, remises and forever discharges the Landlord~~, and his employees and agents~~, from any claims, causes of action or lawsuits arising out of the use of the Property the Tenant has now ~~or may have in the future~~ and is currently aware of.

D. DEALING WITH INDUSTRY FORMS

There are times when documents are presented in a format that makes it look like they cannot be edited, but the reality is there is no reason why you can't change them. Examples of those types of documents are the listing agreement forms and real estate purchase and sale agreement forms that are drafted by trade associations in the real estate industry for use in residential real estate transactions. Those forms may be popular but there is nothing "standard" about them; they were drafted for the people the trade represents. Brokers represent sellers so most realtor generated forms are drafted primarily to represent sellers. If you represent a buyer, there will likely be some changes you will want to make.

So, if you get something like a listing agreement for a residential property in a computerized format that cannot easily be revised, one option you have is to print the document out and then hand write or type the edits on the hard copy before the document is signed. That would be very "old school." If the signing is being done online, another option is to add the changes as an addendum to the document, make sure the document incorporates the addendum by reference, and have the parties also sign the addendum. Here is an example:

Addendum to Limited Listing Agreement
Concerning 123 Black Acre, Alachua, FL

Notwithstanding anything to the contrary in the Listing Agreement (the Agreement) executed on ______ ___, 20___ by and between Realty Corp. (the Broker) and Bob and Mary Smith (the Sellers) concerning the property located at 123 Black Acre, Alachua, Florida (the Property), the parties agree as follows:
The sales commission referred to in the Agreement will be due and payable if, as and when the sale of the Property to the Buyers closes and the deed to the Property is transferred to the Buyers, and not otherwise.

Executed as of this ___ day of _________, 20___.

_______________	_______________
Bob Smith, Seller	Realty Corp. By: [Name][Title]
_______________	
Mary Smith, Seller	

There are always opportunities to add value by revising the documents to better protect your client's interests. Follow the protocols in the agreement; and make it easy for the other side to see what you are asking for and make the requested change. If the original drafter represented the other side, then he drafted the document to advance his client's interests, not yours. As a result, there will always be changes you can make to better serve your client. Take advantage of those opportunities whenever you can. Advance the client's interests by qualifying the language, imposing conditions, and limiting the scope of provisions.

Practice Exercise

Revise the Construction Loan Agreement at the end of this Handbook to better advance the borrower's interests in the transaction. For example,

a. Qualify appropriate representations "to the best of the Borrower's knowledge."
b. Obligate the lender to be reasonable in its requirements and the borrower to do work reasonably satisfactory to the Lender.
c. Consent should not be unreasonably withheld, conditioned or delayed, and costs should also be reasonable.
d. Revise overbroad language to make it narrower.
e. Appropriately condition the exercise of rights affecting the borrower.

Answers to Practice Exercise

See the Construction Loan Agreement "Revised to Better Reflect Borrower's Interests" at the end of this Handbook.

Chapter Eleven
Negotiating Conctract Provisions

Negotiating contract provisions is very different than negotiating something like the settlement of a case. For one thing, there are no dollar amounts to deal with. Also, the process is less adversarial. In litigation, if the settlement falls through, you just go back to fighting it out in court. If you are trying to document a transaction and the negotiations fall through, the transaction doesn't happen. That not only means both sides are upset at you and the other lawyer; it also likely means neither of you get paid. Clients like deal makers, not deal killers. Plus, transactional lawyers often collect their fee from the proceeds of the transaction. So, you never want to let the deal fall through because you and the other lawyer couldn't figure out a reasonable way to document the terms. You need to be a good negotiator. And to do that you need to get prepared before you start negotiating; and adopt a strategy for getting what you really want. But never be a deal killer. Always be a deal maker.

A. Be Prepared

Before you start the negotiating make sure you are prepared. Don't try to do it before you are ready. If the other attorney calls and catches you off guard, tell him you are busy with another project and will call back. Don't let the other side dictate when the negotiations happen.

Ideally, you would have the other attorney come to your office to talk about the revisions. The problem is the other attorney likely wants you to come to his office. Plus, both sides want to get through the process as efficiently as possible, so most negotiations end up happening over the phone.

To prepare, make sure you have an explanation for each change you are requesting and a good argument for why it should be made. Also, make sure you have one or more back up positions. As an example, you might want to change the language to say the work will be done "to the satisfaction of" your client. But, as a backup, you might also be willing to agree to having the work done "to the reasonable satisfaction of" your client.

B. DEVELOP A STRATEGY

You should come up with a strategy for the negotiations. First find out who you will be dealing with. Google the lawyer on the other side and see what her background is. Maybe ask some associates who might know her what her style is. And do the same thing for the client on the other side. Anything you can find out about the parties could be helpful to you in negotiations.

Then strategize about how you want to handle the negotiations. Do you want to put some "throwaways" on the table, and then try to get what you want by giving up the "throwaways" in exchange for what you really want? Do you want to get the client involved and play "god cop; bad cop" with one of you as the good cop and the other as the bad cop? How about testing the water with some relatively unimportant provisions to find out how the other side negotiates, then move on to more important provisions? He may be a haggler or he may be someone who refuses to change anything. Better to know which before you get to the important issues.

Also, think about what leverage your client has. For example, in a financial transaction, the party putting the most money in the deal usually has the most leverage. But that is not always true. There are other interests besides financial interests that you can appeal to. Market forces may also determine who has the most leverage. If you are doing a transaction for the purchase of real estate, and the market is hot, then the seller likely has the most leverage. But, again, that doesn't mean you can't negotiate. You just need a good strategy.

C. DON'T BE A DEAL KILLER

In complex transactions there are often multiple attorneys revising a document. Everyone has to advance their client's interests, but everyone also has to work together to get the deal done. You want to be assertive and persuasive about the changes you request. You don't want to meekly submit some comments and then not even follow up to find out if any were acceptable to the other side. But you never want to get the reputation for being a deal killer. Everyone has to get along for the deal to happen. So, when you are advocating for a particular revision, be sensitive to the other interests involved and look for ways to compromise.

Most attorneys conduct themselves in a professional manner, as the rules of ethics require. But you may nonetheless encounter someone who is difficult to deal with. If you do, don't let him get to you. Know what gets under your skin and make an extra effort to stay under control when someone is pushing your buttons. If you get emotional, the other guy wins. So, stay professional. Try not to let things escalate. And let it go, like water off a duck's back.

Also, know how to deal with a bully. If, for example, the lawyers representing the big banks are pushing the smaller lenders around, it may help for the clients to talk directly. In litigation, the ethical rules prohibit you from contacting the client on the other side. But in transactional practice, the clients are often directly involved in negotiations. Be aware of who is controlling the negotiations. If the lawyer is the problem, continuing to deal with him may not be the best strategy.

Conduct your negotiations with the mindset that you are part of a team of professionals in charge of making the deal happen. There is seldom any harm done by opening your mouth and asking for a change in the language. If you represent a small player in a big project, you may need to choose your battles more carefully than you would otherwise. But you still need to say something, if for no other reason than to justify your existence. No one expects you to be a wallflower. Lawyers are not wallflowers. But you are also not a litigator concerned only with advocating your client's position. You need to be assertive, but you also need to compromise. You need to be an advocate, but you also need to be a deal maker, not a deal killer. If you are good at doing that, your services will always be in demand.

Chapter Twelve
Closing the Deal

I've been hired to draft a lot of documents, but I don't think there has ever been a time when my job wasn't also to get the documents signed and the deal done. Sometimes you just need a signature, but more often there is money to collect as well. If the signer is signing for an entity, you should always get some verification of the signer's authority. If the deal is complex enough, that will be just part of the closing agenda and due diligence process that precedes the actual signing of the documents. And if all goes well, don't forget to follow-up with the client and make sure the door is open for her to refer more work your way.

A. Get the Documents Signed and Collect the Money

The last step in drafting, just like the first step (getting up to speed) has little to do with drafting itself. It is diligently following-up and getting the deal closed. You would be surprised how many times a project "falls through the cracks," especially when you are busy, and your attention is called to other bigger and better things.

And it isn't just the signing you have to get done. If the agreement involves a deposit that is supposed to be collected at closing, your job is to get the money and make sure it goes where it is supposed to go. If you don't do that, there could be hell to pay. If there is a breach by one of the parties later on, and the other party's remedy is to keep the deposit, that party isn't going to be happy to find out you never got it.

B. Verify Authority to Sign for an Entity

If one of the signers is signing on behalf of an entity, you should confirm that person is actually authorized to sign. The most common way of doing that is to require a clerk's certificate and resolutions. The clerk's certificate identifies the signer and the signer's title, and authenticates the attached resolutions which confirm the deal is authorized and the signer is authorized to sign on behalf of the entity. Here is an example for a corporation:

SECRETARY'S CERTIFICATE

The undersigned, on behalf of Cigars for Everyone, Inc., a Florida corporation (the "Corporation") and not individually, certifies that:

1. Attached to this certificate as Exhibit A is a true, correct and complete copy of the Action of Directors at a Meeting of the Directors of the Corporation, duly adopted by the Directors on April 12, 2020, which Action has not been revoked, modified, amended, or rescinded and is in full force and effect as of the date of this certificate (the "Action").
2. The Corporation is a non-profit corporation legally existing and in good standing under the laws of the State of Florida, as of the date of this certificate, and has the power, authority and legal right to enter into, and to execute, deliver, and perform, the obligations under the documents listed in the Action.
3. The following persons have been duly elected and qualified, and on the date hereof are officers of the Corporation, holding the respective offices set opposite their names:

Name	Title
Sam Zapata	President
Eileen Zapata	Secretary

The undersigned, has, on behalf of the Corporation, executed this certificate on this 22nd day of April, 2020.

____

Eileen Zapata, Secretary

Exhibit A

ACTIONS OF DIRECTORS BY WRITTEN CONSENT

CIGARS FOR EVERYONE, INC.

MEETING: April 12, 2020

Pursuant to the Articles of Organization and By-Laws of Cigars for Everyone, Inc., a Florida corporation (the "Corporation"), the Directors of the Corporation do adopt the following resolutions and agree to the taking of the actions set forth below:

RESOLVED: That the Corporation is empowered, authorized, and directed to take all action and execute and deliver any documents necessary or proper to direct, complete, carry out, consummate and effectuate the transfer, conveyance, or sale of the project located on the property at 101 University Avenue, Gainesville, Florida (the "Property").

RESOLVED: That the President of the Corporation, Sam Zapata, be, and is, empowered, authorized, and directed in the name of and on behalf of the Corporation to take all action and execute and deliver any documents necessary or proper to direct, complete, carry out, consummate, and effectuate the transfer, conveyance or sale of the Property to the University of Florida, including, without limitation, a quitclaim deed of the Property from the Corporation to the University of Florida, a Settlement Statement, 1099 Form and Property Owner's Affidavit.

C. CREATE A CLOSING AGENDA

If the deal is something like a commercial loan for the construction of a multi-unit building, then the process will likely involve the creation of a closing agenda, which is a list of due diligence items that need to be produced, reviewed, and approved before the documents are actually signed and the deal closed. Here is an example of a short closing checklist:

Closing Checklist

A $1,000,000.00 Mortgage loan from Fictitious Bank (Lender) to Borrower Corporation (Borrower). Items marked B are to be submitted by the Borrower. Items marked L are the responsibility of Lender.

A. Organization and Authority of Borrower

1. Articles of Organization, and any amendments — B
2. Bylaws, and any amendments — B
3. Current Legal Existence/Good Standing Certificate — B
4. Evidence of Authority for Transactions (resolutions/incumbency) — B

B. Loan Documents

1. $1,000,000.00 Promissory Note — L
2. Mortgage and Security Agreement — L
3. Loan Agreement with all Exhibits attached — L
4. UCC Financing Statements — L

C. Title Insurance Matters

1. Copy of Title Insurance Commitment provided to Lender — B
2. Title Exception Documents — B

D. Legal Opinions

1. Opinion of Borrower's Counsel as to execution, delivery, validity and enforceability of Loan Documents — B
2. Opinion of Borrower's Counsel as to compliance with building, zoning, and subdivision laws and regulations — B

E. Other Documents

1. Copy of Building Permit — B
2. Environmental Assessment — B
3. Project Development Budget — B
4. Contract with General Contractor — B

As you can see, in a larger deal it is typical not to just rely on the clerk's certificate and resolutions to verify the signer's authority. The corporation's articles and bylaws are requested and reviewed. Those organizational documents will typically indicate who has what authority. An attorney's opinion of enforceability is also required. The opinion will state that, in the attorney's opinion, the signers are authorized, and the documents are enforceable. Also, the lender typically requires title insurance, insuring the priority and enforceability of the mortgage securing the loan.

The agenda also helps to keep everyone focused and on track in a large commercial project involving a lot of attorneys. Using e-mail helps keep people in the loop too. At the beginning of every closing I handled, one of the first things I did was get everyone's e-mail address. E-mail is an effective way to keep everyone in the loop and deliver copies of documents, drafts, and other closing materials.

I used to also participate in periodic conference calls for the closings I was involved in. If I were doing closings today, I'd do the conferences online with a service like Zoom, Uberconference or Skype. The advantage of an online conference is that you can put a document on the screen during the conference so everyone else can see it. You can revise the document in real time as various modifications are discussed. And you can keep a recording of what was said and done by the parties and their attorneys while the conference took place, assuming everyone consents to being recorded.

D. FOLLOW UP AFTER THE CLOSING

After the deal is done, it is usually counsel's responsibility to distribute to the parties either the original, signed documents or copies of the signed documents. In the old days, attorneys would distribute a closing "bible" containing all the relevant documents. Today you will most likely send out a CD containing pdfs of the same documents. When you send that package out to the client, I would also recommend sending the client a cover letter highlighting any deadlines or other important provisions in the agreement the client will need to remember. Put together a nice organized package so the client can see what she paid for and thank her for the opportunity to be of service. The end of every transaction, assuming all went well, is a good time to continue developing your relationship with the client.

Law is a service industry. You can't save the world if the world does not want to hire you to do the work. In the same way that you should always look for opportunities to add value to a deal, you should also be on the lookout for opportunities to further develop your relationships with clients. As long as you have clients, you will never have trouble finding a job.

Chapter Thirteen
Ethical Issues in Contract Drafting

Ethical issues are not easy to deal with in a transactional practice. Most of the ethical rules are for litigators not transactional attorneys, so there is often not much guidance. But there are still plenty of ethical pitfalls for transactional attorneys. And they are even more difficult to deal with when you are just starting out. If you commit malpractice you may lose your job, but professional liability insurance will likely cover the loss, assuming you have it. If you commit a violation of the rules of ethics, you could lose your license. So, the stakes are high!

Suppose you are working in a law firm, helping a senior partner close a loan. You send a draft loan agreement to borrower's counsel. Unknown to you, the document contains metadata showing the deletion of an "ipso facto" clause in a prior version. Borrower's counsel checks the metadata and requests the same change for his client's documents. The partner tells you to go ahead and delete the clause. He says the bank includes it because some borrowers don't realize it's unenforceable. Then he tells you to hurry up and get the loan closed. You are rushing when you print out the documents, and accidentally print out the original unchanged version for the borrower to sign. After the closing, the senior partner catches the mistake and tells you to correct it by attaching the signature page to the revised version. He also sees you forgot to get the signature on the mortgage notarized. But you able to correct that mistake as well; you take the document to a notary and have him notarize it after the fact. You then have the loan documents compiled and bound, and send them to the client with a letter explaining the substantive requirements in the documents. You aren't in the office when the letter is typed up, so you ask your paralegal to sign your name and send it out.

How many ethical issues do you see?

I'm sure every law student knows you can't defraud your own client or lie to the court. Among other things, attorneys are prohibited in the ethical rules from engaging "in conduct involving dishonesty, fraud, deceit, or misrepresentation...." *E.g.*, Florida Rules of Professional Conduct, Rule 4-8.4(c). But there are a lot of subtle ways you could find yourself doing something in connection with your drafting that could be considered dishonest.

Is it ethical, for example, to include in a contract a provision you know is unenforceable, like an "ipso facto" clause (entitling the lender to call the loan if the borrower files a bankruptcy petition), for the purpose of deceiving a party as to his rights? *E.g.*, Florida Rules of Professional Conduct, 4-1.2(d)("A lawyer shall not counsel a client to engage, or assist a client, in conduct that the lawyer knows or reasonably should know is criminal or fraudulent."); *See*, Alexandra Sickler, *Ethics in Contract Drafting*, 64 Gavel 10.

You probably know what metadata is (information attached to a document that is not visible on the face of the document); but are you may not be in the habit of scrubbing the metadata from your word documents before you provide them to the client or a third party? What if you circulate a set of loan documents you drafted and accidentally include in the metadata confidential information about the client? It is clear an attorney has an ethical obligation to keep client information confidential. *E.g.*, Florida Rules of Professional Conduct, 4-1.6(a). Are you in violation of the rule if you accidentally reveal that confidential information to a third party? *See e.g.*, Florida Rules of Professional Conduct, 4-1.6(e) ("A lawyer must make reasonable efforts to prevent the inadvertent or unauthorized disclosure of, or unauthorized access to, information relating to the representation of a client").

What if you fail to keep track of the final version of a document and accidentally arrange for the signing of an early draft at the closing? You are implicitly representing the document is the final version by producing it at the closing, but the misrepresentation is not intentional. Again, does it matter that you did it by accident? *See e.g.*, Florida Rules of Professional Conduct, Rule 4-1.1 (Attorneys must also "provide competent representation," which requires "the legal knowledge, skill, thoroughness, and preparation reasonably necessary for the representation.")

I think it's a clear ethical violation to have a client sign a blank signature page, and then substitute the document later. If the client signed a blank page and then you made it look like the client signed the document you attached, that is clearly deceitful. But what if you substitute one document for a revised version after the document is signed? Does it matter whether the client knows about the substitution, and consents to the new document's terms, or whether the changes are material, or only affect the rights of another party to the document? The client still didn't do what it has been made to look like the client did, right?

What if a senior attorney tells you to do it? Is that an excuse? "A lawyer is bound by the Rules of Professional Conduct notwithstanding that the lawyer acted at the direction of another person." *E.g.*, Florida Rules of Professional Conduct, Rule 4-5.2(a). So, what would you do? Would you refuse? Or is there some better way of handling the situation?

It isn't unusual for parties to separately sign duplicate originals of a contract if they are in two different places when the closing occurs. And there is no problem with the closing attorney subsequently combining the signature pages to form one fully signed document. What is the difference between that situation and the one in the hypothetical?

If a client has already signed a document, can the attorney have it notarized after the fact? The notary's jurat[16] usually states that the signer "subscribed before me." Subscribed means signed, so isn't the notary attesting to a misrepresentation if the signer didn't actually sign in front of the notary?

And finally, is it o.k. to have your paralegal sign your name to a cover letter? If the letter just says, "Enclosed please find copies of the documents," that's one thing. But the paralegal's identity and nonlawyer status should still be disclosed. If the letter discusses the substantive content of the documents, that's likely different. Among other things, a lawyer may be aiding in the unauthorized practice of law by allowing a nonlawyer to sign a letter containing legal advice. *See*, Florida Rules of Professional Conduct, 4-5.5(b)(2) (A nonlawyer may not "hold out to the public or otherwise represent that the lawyer is admitted to practice in Florida.").

I remember my ethics professor in law school saying "Your license is your ticket to practice law. Whatever you do, don't do anything that could put your ticket in jeopardy." Unfortunately, when you are really busy and under a lot of stress, there are shortcuts you might be tempted to take that might seem perfectly innocent at the time. But later, with 20/20 hindsight, what you did might also be characterized as inappropriate. Despite the rush of activity, you still have to pay close attention and stay on top of what you are doing to avoid ending up on the wrong side of an ethics complaint.

---

16 Jurat is short for the Latin word "Juratum," meaning"it has been sworn."Merriam-Webster, Collegiate Dictionary (11th ed. 2014). A notary's jurat will typically say something like "sworn to (or affirmed) and subscribed before me this ____ day of ____, 20__, by (name of person making statement)."

Chapter Fourteen
Drafting a Contract Amendment

There is one more skill that I think is important to know if you are going to practice in this area, and that is how to draft a contract amendment. For a variety of reasons, you may need to go back and change something in a contract you have already drafted. One party or the other may have changed their practices. Something about the way the deal was originally planned may not be working as well as it could. Or, the parties may want to expand what they had originally contemplated doing. When this happens, drafting a new agreement may be an option. But often the preferred method is to leave what already exists in place and just provide for the new terms. If you need to draft a contract amendment, here is a quick outline of how to do it.

The first thing you need to think about when drafting an amendment is whether it is better to amend the document or just start over with a new agreement. The one big advantage of amending is it doesn't give the other party an opportunity to renegotiate any of the provisions that aren't changing. But there are other legal issues to consider as well. If the document is a security instrument, the client may lose the priority of their interest by starting over. So, it may be better to amend. If the document is a negotiable instrument, amending may destroy the negotiability of the instrument. So, it may be better to start over and re-do the original document. Consider those issues first. If an amendment makes sense, then start drafting.

Start off with a title and exordium, referring to the original agreement, like this:

AMENDMENT TO APARTMENT LEASE

This Amendment to Apartment Lease (Amendment) dated January 25, 2019, is by and between South Tower Management Corp., a Florida Corporation having an office at 123 Main Street in Jacksonville, Florida (Landlord) and William Lancaster III, an individual having a residence at 23 Beach Avenue, Apt. 567, Jacksonville Beach, Florida (Tenant). The parties mutually agree as follows:

Then draft a background section explaining what happened and why the parties are amending the original document.

1. Background of Amendment

A. On January 2, 2015 Landlord and Tenant entered into an apartment lease for the property located at 31 West Street, Unit 310, Gainesville, Florida (the Lease).
B. The Lease was for a term of four (4) years beginning on January 2, 2015 and ending on January 1, 2019; and the monthly rent provided for in the Lease was $1,500 per month.
C. The Tenant now desires to extend the term of the Lease; and the Landlord is willing to extend the term at a higher rental rate.

Accordingly, the parties mutually agree as follows:

If you want to use the defined terms in the original lease, then consider adding a statement like this: "Capitalized terms not otherwise defined in this Amendment have the same meanings as provided in the Lease."

After you have completed the background section, explain what each change is, as though you are editing the original document. In other words, reference the section to change, delete the old language, and insert the new language, like this:

2. Changes to Lease

A. Section 3 of the Lease (Term of Rental) is deleted and replaced with the following:

"3. Term of Rental

The term of the rental is for four (4) years beginning on January 2, 2019 and ending on January 1, 2023."

B. Section 4(a) of the Lease (Payment of Rent) is deleted and replaced with the following:

"(a) Payment of Rent

On or before the first day of each month, the Tenant will pay the Landlord rent in the amount of two thousand dollars ($2,000) per month."

Once you have made all the changes, finish with a reiteration of the rest of the contract, a testimonium, and signature lines.

3. Remainder of Lease

All other terms and conditions of the Lease remain in full force and effect.

Executed by the parties as of the date above.

Landlord	Tenant
______________________	______________________
South Tower Mgmt Corp. By: [Name] [Title]	William Lancaster III

Now you know how to draft a contract from scratch, revise a form document, negotiate terms, and close a deal. We have discussed the ethical issues you might run into in the process, plus how to amend a contract after the fact. Now let's look at how technology has affected contract drafting.

Chapter Fifteen
Using Computers to Draft Documents

In the introduction to this book I wrote a brief timeline of how contracts have been created over the years. Today we are transitioning from a period when paper was king to a digital age when everything is recorded in computer files. When personal computers first became popular, attorneys used them to replace a typewriter and a filing cabinet. But now more and more of the actual drafting of documents is being done by computer.[17]

When I first started doing transactional work, it was common practice for the closing attorney to deliver to the parties a "closing binder" after the transaction was completed. The closing binder consisted of copies of all the documents and a table of contents (a revised version of the closing agenda), nicely "velo" bound together.[18] Later the practice changed to providing the same content on a computer disc (cd). Cd's save a lot of paper and space, but there are also disadvantages to storing documents in digital form. CD's replaced floppy disks which are now extinct. And CD's are being replaced more and more by flash drives, so CD's may soon be extinct as well. I have old files on my computer that I can no longer open because they were drafted with software that is no longer in use. Say what you want about paper and other primitive forms of storing information, but there are cave paintings made by Neanderthals 64,000 years ago that you can still read.

Today, computers are not only used to store documents, computers are also used to draft documents. One type of program is just a form filler. The user inputs factual information and the program inserts that information into appropriate blanks in form documents. But other programs are more sophisticated. For example, there are programs that will not only fill in the blanks, but also decide what types of provisions to use depending upon what the facts are. So, the software might ask whether the loan is to be a recourse loan or a nonrecourse loan. Depending upon the answer, the software will insert the provisions applicable to a recourse loan or the provisions applicable to a nonrecourse loan,

17 Beverly Rich, *How AI is Changing Contracts*, Harvard Business Review (2018).

18 Velo binding is an inexpensive and widely available type of book binding.

and then fill in the blanks in those provisions. The software might also ask for the identity of the borrower. If the borrower is a partnership, then the program will add provisions appropriate for a partnership. If the borrower is a corporation, the program will add provisions appropriate for a corporation.[19]

Banks use this kind of software to generate residential loan documents with the usual Fannie Mae forms. Brokers use this type of software to generate purchase and sale agreements and other simple documents for use in residential real estate transactions. Similar programs are available to consumers. Nolo sells a popular program called WillMaker that will walk a non-lawyer through the process of drafting a last will and testament. Rocket Lawyer, LegalZoom and Law Depot are online services that help consumers and small businesses draft simple legal documents. Programs like HotDocs, XpressDox, and Contract Express help lawyers to produce a first draft of more complex documents. And programs like LegalSifter and LawGeex use artificial intelligence to help attorneys review existing contracts.[20] If I were in law school today, I would consider learning how to use that type of software and adding my proficiency with it to my resume.

Does all this mean we don't need lawyers? No. These programs make the process more efficient, but they don't eliminate the need for good lawyers. You should be aware of them because, as a practical matter, you have to be able to do better than they can do. If the client can go online and print out a document that is just as good as the one you drafted, then the client no longer needs your services. It is more convenient, less expensive and less time-consuming to have a computer draft a document than to meet with an attorney and wait for the attorney to send you a draft (and a bill). As a result, the product the attorney produces must always be better than any computer can do.

It also used to be that documents were executed in a closing in an attorney's office, but that is changing too. More and more documents are executed online with electronic signatures.[21] For example, programs called DotLoop, DocuSign

---

19 For a good overview of modern-day contract drafting programs and their limitations see, Kathryn D. Betts and Kyle R. Jaep, *The Dawn of Fully Automated Contract Drafting: Machine Learning Breathes Life into a Decades-Old Promise*, 15 Duke L. & Tech. Rev. (2017); *see also* Irene Ng (Huang Ying), *The Art of Contract Drafting in the Age of Artificial Intelligence: A Comparative Study Based on US, UK and Austrian Law*, TTLF Working Papers No. 26, Stanford-Vienna Transatlantic Technology Law Forum (2017).

20 For a discussion of contract drafting scholar Ken Adams's involvement in LegalSifter *see*, Jamie Hwang, *Legal Writing Pro is Helping Teach AI to Draft Contracts*, ABA Law Journal, Legal Rebels (September 12, 2018).

21 The validity and enforceability of electronic contracts and electronic signatures is assured by the

and HelloSign enable brokers to have some real estate documents signed online. Someday we may find ourselves relying on a retinal scan or some other biometric measure to show that an agreement was made.[22] For now it is often still necessary that a deed be signed in person, on paper, and in the presence of a notary for a real estate closing to occur. And banks still typically insist that their loan documents be signed in person. So, attorneys still conduct in person closings, although they may happen less often.

Attorneys are using technology more and more, just like everyone else. But in the most important respects, the attorney's role remains unchanged. When you represent a client, the client is not paying you to obtain a form document or fill in the blanks and print one out, and then witness your signature. The client is paying you to think. It is important that you have the skill to express the client's agreement in a clear, complete, and accurate manner. But substance is what matters most. And that means using the knowledge and training you began to acquire in law school and continued to build on in practice to advance the client's goals and protect the client's interests. Computers may make the process more efficient. But until the day comes when a computer can go through law school and think like a lawyer, there will always be a need for the minds of people like us. There will always be a place for smart, knowledgeable lawyers who draft well. Keep learning as much as you can. Practice. And seek perfection in everything you write. Good luck!

---

federal Electronic Signatures in Global and National Commerce Act, 15 U.S.C. § 7001(a), and state Uniform Electronic Transactions Acts. E.g., Fla. Stat. § 668.50(7).

22 Suraiya Jabin & Farhana Zareen, *Biometric Signature Verification*, International Journal of Biometrics (January 2015).

ABOUT THE AUTHOR

Ben Fernandez teaches Legal Drafting and Legal Research and Writing at the University of Florida Levin College of Law. He had previously taught Legal Methods, Legal Research and Objective Writing, Lawyering Process for Litigation Practice, and Transactional Drafting at Florida Coastal School of Law. Also, he worked as an adjunct professor teaching Legal Writing at Northeastern University School of Law in Boston, and Business Law at Cape Cod Community College.

Ben has twenty-five years of experience practicing law in Massachusetts. He represented financial institutions and government finance agencies in commercial and residential finance transactions. He had his own practice in Plymouth, Massachusetts for ten years. Before that, he practiced law in the city of Boston for fifteen years. He worked as in-house counsel for a state-sponsored affordable housing finance agency, managed the business department of a prominent minority-owned firm, and was an associate at two large Boston law firms.

Also, Ben served on the Board of Directors for Habitat for Humanity of Greater Plymouth, Massachusetts. He was a volunteer teacher in Junior Achievement's Financial Literacy program, and a regular speaker at Homebuyer Education Workshops sponsored by South Shore Housing and Housing Assistance Corporation on Cape Cod.

Ben has an LL.M. from Boston University School of Law, as well as a J.D. from Northeastern University School of Law and a B.A. from Cornell University.

INDEX

APPENDIX

Flowchart for Drafting Contract Provisions

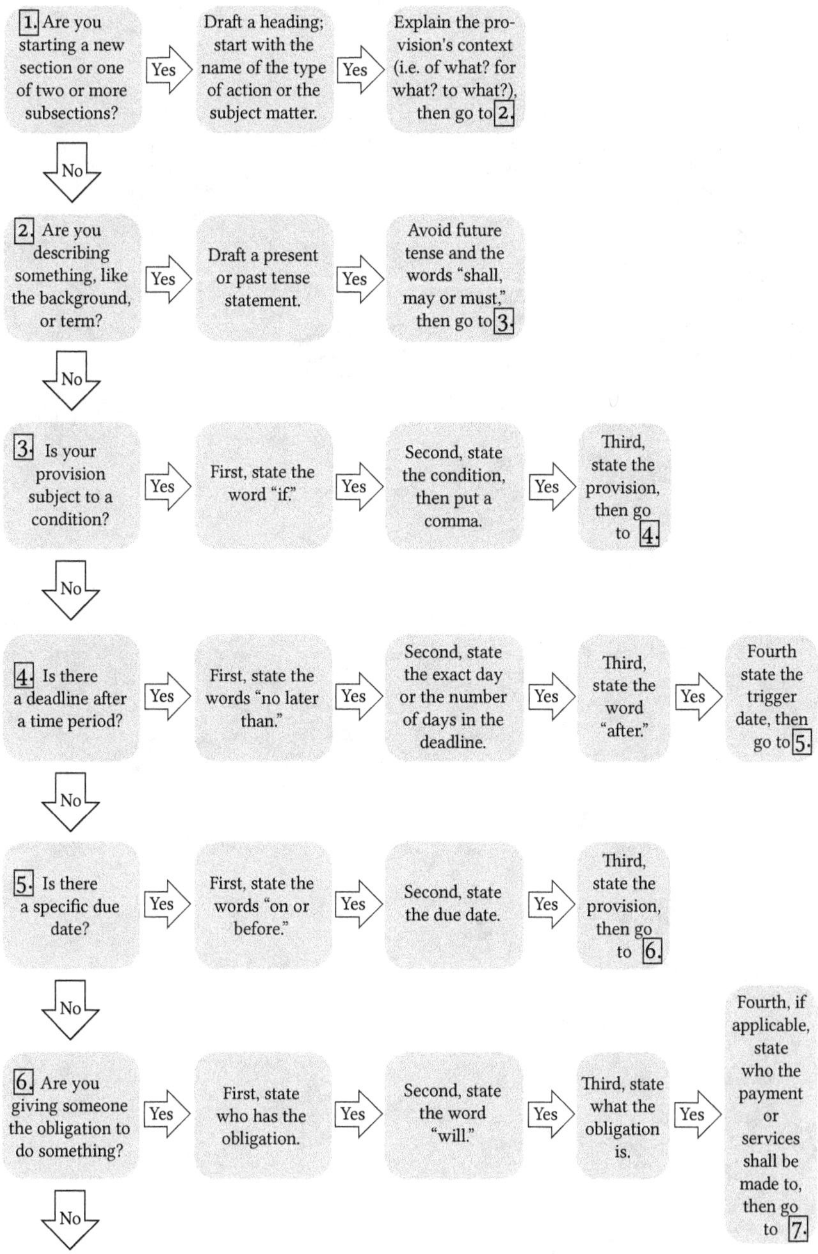

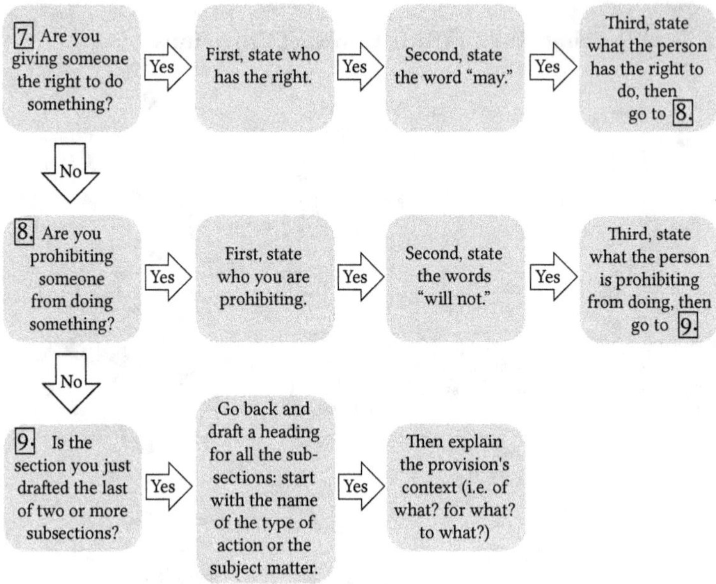

Prof. Ben L. Fernandez
Legal Drafting

Conctract Drafting Checklist

1. Begin your provisions with the name of a party, not a non-party or a thing.

2. Use "shall" or "will" to obligate the party to act.

3. Use "shall not" or "will not" to prohibit the party from acting.

4. Use "may" to give the party the right to act.

5. Don't use any other words for obligations, prohibitions or rights. (i.e. don't use "agrees," "has discretion," "is prohibited," "is required to," etc.).

6. Draft descriptions as past or present tense statements. There is seldom a need to use future tense in an agreement.

7. Make the subject of sentences the relevant party; use active voice.

8. Make sentences complete (state who, what, to whom, when and how, if applicable).

9. Omit legalese and other needless jargon.

10. Proofread for spelling, punctuation, and grammar.

11. Start with a <u>Title</u> identifying the type of contract.

12. Then an <u>Exordium</u> containing the following information (Don't give this section a heading): effective date, name of parties, address and state of organization, if applicable, reference to title, and

expression of intent to be bound by the contract's provisions (i.e. words of agreement).

13. Use short forms to refer to the parties and the agreement (put in parenthesis; start with a capital letter).

14. Use a heading for each subsequent section of contract (except for the testimonium and the signature lines at the end); subsections should also have headings. Each heading and subsection should be numbered or lettered, if there is more than one.

15. Draft a Background of Agreement section, if applicable. Recite business or nature of parties, history and reasons for transaction, or description of subject matter. Use descriptive statements.

16. Draft the Core Covenant. Obligate each side to complete their part of the bargain; express the core exchange of promises between the parties. (Don't label this section "Core Covenant;" Do use "will" or "shall").

17. Draft Duration, if applicable. Describe the intended length of the period and state the beginning and ending dates.

18. Draft Supplemental Provisions for the details of the agreement. Expand upon the services to be provided and payments to be made; express the details of when, where, and how. (Don't label this section "Supplemental Provisions" or "Obligations of X" and "Obligations of Y;" Do use "will," "shall" or "may").

19. Payment Clauses. Indicate who payment is to, when it is due, how it is to be made, and what payment is for.

20. Time Clauses. Use "on" for due dates, "before," "on or before," "after," "on or after," "no later than," or "no earlier than" for deadlines. Make sure the "trigger date" is clear. Use days instead of weeks or months.

21. Conditions. Use "if," "unless," or "except." If a time clause modifies a condition, place the time clause within the phrase of the condition the time clause refers to.

22. Insurance. Use "will maintain" or "shall maintain." Identify the type of insurance and amount of coverage. Name the other party as beneficiary / loss payee. Require the party to provide proof of insurance.

23. Indemnity. Use "will" or "shall." Identify the person the clause applies to. Specify the items indemnified. Indicate if negligence and attorney's fees are included. State any exceptions.

24. Termination / Cancellation. Use "may." Cancellation if breach; otherwise termination. Specify method of termination.

25. Modification. Descriptive policy that modifications are valid only if done with a written record signed by all parties.

26. Integration / Merger. Describe the parol evidence rule. Contract is integrated, complete, and final. Prior agreements are merged, superseded.

27. Forum Selection / Venue. Describe forum choice. Make the clause mandatory and exclusive. Make the clause conspicuous. Delineate the scope of the clause.

28. Applicable Law. Describe choice for applicable law. State what law applies to determine the scope of the choice of law clause. State what law applies to a claim based on a tort or statute.

29. Testimonium. "Executed by the parties as of the date written above." Do not use legalese. (Do not give this section a heading).

30. Signature Lines. Include the name for an individual (personal liability); "by," "name," and "title" if a representative (no personal liability).

Laptop Purchase Agreement
Transcript of Client Intake

Fernandez: Good morning.

Lancaster: Good morning, Ben. How are you?

Fernandez: I am well, Margaret. Thank you.

Lancaster: So, what brings you in today?

Fernandez: Well, I've been working on an agreement with Apple computer. I want you to document it.

Lancaster: Wonderful. Is the agreement with the University or just the Law School?

Fernandez: I think it should be with the Levin College of Law.

Lancaster: We've worked with Apple before. I think the legal name is "Apple, Inc." and they are out of California, right?

Fernandez: Yes, they are a Delaware corporation located in California. The address is One Apple Park Way in Cupertino.

Lancaster: I've been there. The giant circular building?

Fernandez: That's it. Anyway, we went there to work with Apple to address a student / teacher issue we've been dealing with. Students like to use laptops in class, but teachers find them distracting. Many of the law school professors have outright banned them.

Lancaster: I see the issue. But it's not really the computer that is the problem; it is the internet, right?

Fernandez: Exactly. As it turns out, Apple has people working on the same issue: making a classroom-friendly computer product. You know, Apple has a lot of interest in education and working with teachers to assimilate computers into the classroom.

Lancaster: I know. So, did you come up with a solution?

Fernandez: I think so. Apple is going to develop a line of classroom approved computers for us, and we are going to give them to all the entering 1L students.

Lancaster: Wow. A free laptop for every student. Sounds like a good marketing idea.

Fernandez: It is, isn't it? We'll raise the tuition $1,000 to compensate, but that's another issue.

Lancaster: So, what is a classroom approved computer?

Fernandez: Well, it's basically the MacBook Air model with certain modifications.

Lancaster: How is it different?

Fernandez: First and foremost, it is Wi-fi and Bluetooth disabled. In other words, it doesn't have either of those features, and it is made so neither can be added. That's important, so we want them to put in writing in the contract that these computers cannot be used for internet access.

Lancaster: I guess that takes care of internet surfing and e-mailing in class.

Fernandez: Right. Second, it is preloaded with E-books for all required courses. We've already given the books to Apple, so they can upload them to each laptop.

Lancaster: What a great idea. No more lugging around a backpack full of books. The students will love that.

Fernandez: Third, in terms of software, the laptops will also come with Microsoft Word, Acrobat Reader, Dragon Naturally Speaking, and Grammarly. But programs like Safari, Mail, Messages, iTunes, and Facetime will all be deleted.

Lancaster: Hmm. I've never heard of Dragon Naturally Speaking. What is that? Dictation software?

Fernandez: Yes, it's fantastic. You should try it in your practice. Once you get used to using it, you will wonder how you did without it.

Lancaster: O.k., is that it?

Fernandez: No, one more thing. The enclosure for each computer will be blue on the bottom and orange on the top, and the gator logo will also be on the top. We saw a prototype yesterday. It was great. The gator lights up when you turn the computer on.

Lancaster: Wow. I think these will be a hit. So, is UF committing to buy a certain number of the laptops?

Fernandez: Yes. For starters, we are buying 250 laptops for $1,000 each. So that's $250,000 total.

Lancaster: That's a lot of laptops!

Fernandez: Well, they will be delivered to the Faculty Lounge in Holland Hall. They should be there by August 1st. If they come early, that's fine. But they have to be there by the 1st so we can get them to the students before classes start.

Lancaster: Do they have to be set up or prepped or anything before the students get them?

Fernandez: No, they are ready to go. Just open the box and plug them in.

Lancaster: Great. How is the University paying? Lump sum? Installments?

Fernandez: Installments. Apple didn't like it, but they agreed to let us pay $6,944.44 per month for three years. Payments are due the first of each month.

Lancaster: Late fee?

Fernandez: No. We decided that if a payment is late, Apple has to give us written notice and one month to cure. If we then make the payment plus simple interest at the default rate of 12% per annum, the breach is cured. But if we don't make the payment within one month, then we have to pay the remaining balance in full.

Lancaster: Two questions. Does the cure period start when the notice is received? And does interest accrue just on the outstanding payment?

Fernandez: Yes, and yes.

Lancaster: O.k.

Fernandez: And the payments are by wire transfer. We'll need wire instructions from Apple to make that happen, so make sure they are obligated to give the instructions before the first payment is due.

Lancaster: Isn't the first payment due when the contract is signed?

Fernandez: No, the payments start when the laptops are delivered.

Lancaster: O.k.

Fernandez: Now, one of the things that was important to Apple was the law school agree to adopt a policy approving the use of these computers in all classes. So, we should probably put that in there somewhere.

Lancaster: O.k. What about repairs and maintenance? How will that work?

Fernandez: A representative of Apple will come to the school once a week during each semester and handle any repair or replacement claims. We will give the representative a table or a booth in the student lounge to work out of. Don't put that in the contract though. Just make sure they are obligated to provide that service.

Lancaster: For how long will Apple provide that service?

Fernandez: Three years from when the computers are delivered.

Lancaster: Will the University pay for the service?

Fernandez: Yes. It's an extra $250 per month, due on the first day of each month. We'll pay the rent by check. And we can terminate at any time. These units should be fairly trouble-free so there may be no need for repairs.

Lancaster: What about notice and an opportunity to cure? Does that apply to the rental period too?

Fernandez: No. They are going to give us a one-week grace period. After that, there is a $25 late fee. And they can cancel the lease if any payment is more than a month overdue. Of course, if they cancel the lease, we still have to continue paying for the computers.

Lancaster: What about a warranty? Is there some type of warranty?

Fernandez: Yes, it is the same for any other MacBook Air. Apple has it on their website. I don't think we need to restate it in the contract.

Lancaster: Yeah, but the law school is not an authorized reseller. Can the students still take advantage of the warranty?

Fernandez: Yes, we talked about that when we were in California. Apple is giving the University the right to transfer the warranty to the students. Also, computers bought or received from the University pursuant to this arrangement will be eligible for participation in Apple's GiveBack Program. You can read about that on the website.

Lancaster: O.k., so even though the school is not an authorized reseller, like a store selling computers to the public, computers received from the school are still covered by the warranty, and they are still eligible for participation in the GiveBack Program.

Fernandez: Correct. But there is a condition.

Lancaster: What?

Fernandez: To obtain warranty coverage for the students, UF has to give Apple the name and address of every student receiving a computer pursuant to this program. The same is true of the GiveBack program.

Lancaster: What else did you talk about when you were in California?

Fernandez: Let's see. We agreed not to sell or give these computers to anyone other than students at UF. Also, Apple agreed we could advertise these computers on campus, as long as we use their marketing materials; and they said they would provide us with what we need.

Lancaster: When do we get the marketing materials?

Fernandez: Within a month after the contract is signed.

Lancaster: It almost sounds like UF will be an agent of Apple.

Fernandez: Apple doesn't want that. In fact, they want the contract to make clear we are not employees or agents.

Lancaster: What if 2Ls and 3Ls want the computers? You said the school was only giving them to first year students, didn't you?

Fernandez: Yes, but 2Ls and 3Ls can also buy them directly from Apple. If they verify their status by providing a student ID, Apple agreed that they will sell them a classroom-approved computer for $1,000. That's the same price we pay.

Lancaster: O.k. You didn't agree to any exculpatory provisions, did you?

Fernandez: We resisted but they wanted an indemnity, so we have to give them one. Draft it narrowly, of course. But we do need to include an indemnity.

Lancaster: Release?

Fernandez: No release. No waiver. Just the indemnity.

Lancaster: What about administrative provisions? I would normally have the parties agree that Florida law applies, and, if there is litigation, it will be commenced in Alachua County.

Fernandez: Good. That's fine. There have also been a lot of side discussions leading up to this agreement. Likely, that will continue. Representatives of each side may also try to decide on changes to the agreement after it is signed. But we want to prevent all that. If it isn't in writing and signed by the parties, it isn't part of the arrangement. And that should be true whether someone claims it was decided before the document was signed or after it was executed. Do you know what I mean?

Lancaster: Yes. I can take care of those issues with a couple standard provisions.

Fernandez: Excellent. I think that's about it.

Lancaster: O.k., I can have a draft for you a week from today. Is that o.k.?

Fernandez: Yes, that's fine. I look forward to reviewing it.

Laptop Purchase Agreement

On April ___, 2019, the University of Florida Levin College of Law, the law school of a public university located at 309 Village Drive, Gainesville, Florida (UF) and Apple, Inc., a Delaware corporation located at One Apple Parkway, Cupertino, California (Apple) enter into this Laptop Purchase Agreement (Agreement). The parties mutually agree as follows:

I. Background of Agreement

A. Development of Laptops

UF students desire to use laptops in class, but professors find them distracting. Many of the law school professors have outright banned them. Apple has been working on a classroom-friendly computer product. Apple is interested in education and working with teachers to assimilate computers into the classroom. Together, UF and Apple have developed a line of classroom computers for UF students to use.

B. Specifications for Laptops

The classroom-approved computers are based on the MacBook Air model with the following modifications:

i. they are Wi-Fi and Bluetooth disabled;

ii. they are preloaded with E-books for all required courses, as well as Microsoft Word, Acrobat Reader, Dragon Naturally Speaking, and Grammarly (Safari, Mail, Messages, iTunes and Facetime are deleted); and

iii. they are in enclosures that are blue on the bottom, orange on the top and have a Gator logo on the top (Classroom Approved Laptops).

II. Purchase of Classroom Approved Laptops

Apple will sell to UF two hundred fifty (250) Classroom Approved Laptops for $1,000 each; and UF will pay Apple a total of $250,000 pursuant to the terms of this Agreement.

III. Payment for Classroom Approved Laptops

a. Payment in Installments
   UF will pay Apple $250,000 in thirty-six (36) equal installments of $6,944.44 each. UF will pay the installments on or before the first day of each month for a period of three (3) years, beginning on August 1, 2019 and ending on July 1, 2022.

b. Notice and Opportunity to Cure
   If UF fails to make any payment on time, Apple will send UF written notice of such failure. If UF fails to cure by making such payment on or before the thirtieth day after UF's receipt of the notice, then UF will immediately pay Apple the remaining balance in full.

c. Method of Payment
   UF will make the payments described in this section by wire transfer. Apple will provide UF with wire instructions no later than thirty (30) days after the day this Agreement is executed.

IV. Delivery of Classroom Approved Laptops

Apple will deliver the two hundred fifty (250) Classroom Approved Laptops to UF at the faculty lounge in Holland Hall on or before August 1, 2019.

V. Repair and Maintenance of Classroom Approved Laptops

a. Provision of Repair Service
   Apple will arrange for a qualified employee of Apple to be present at UF to handle any repair or replacement claims one day per week

during the fall and spring semesters for the three (3) year period beginning on August 1, 2019 and ending on May 31, 2022.

b. Term of Repair Service
   UF will pay Apple two hundred fifty dollars ($250) per month on or before the first day of each month for this repair or replacement service. UF may terminate this service at any time by providing written notice to Apple.

c. Fee for Late Payment
   If UF fails to timely make any payment to Apple, and such failure continues for seven (7) or more days after the date such payment is due, then UF will pay Apple a late fee of twenty-five (25) dollars. If such failure continues for more than thirty (30) days, then Apple may cancel the provision of this service.

d. Method of Payment
   UF will make the payments described in this section by check.

VI. Transfer of Warranty

Although UF is not an authorized reseller, UF may nonetheless transfer to UF's students the warranty on each Classroom Approved Laptop," as long as UF provides Apple with the name and address of every student who receives a Classroom Approved Laptop. Apple will also accept Classroom Approved Laptops purchased by students of UF for participation in Apple's "GiveBack Program," as long as UF provides Apple with the name and address of every student who receives a Classroom Approved Laptop.

VII. Policy for Use of Classroom Approved Laptops

UF will adopt a policy permitting the use of Classroom Approved Laptops in all courses offered by UF.

VIII. Prohibition on Sales Outside UF

UF will not sell or otherwise transfer Classroom Approved Laptops to any person or entity that is not a student of UF.

IX. Marketing of Classroom Approved Laptops

Apple will provide UF with marketing materials for the Classroom Approved Laptops no later than thirty (30) days after this Agreement is executed.

X. Clarification of Status

UF is not an employee or agent of Apple.

XI. Purchase by Upper Level Students

Apple will sell Classroom Approved Laptops to second and third-year students of UF for no more than $1,000 per Classroom Approved Laptop.

XII. Indemnification of Claims

UF will indemnify and hold harmless Apple from and against third party claims arising out of the purchase of Classroom Approved Laptops, but excluding claims based on Apple's own actions or failure to act.

XIII. Merger of Agreement

This Agreement is final and complete. All prior statements, understanding and agreements are merged.

XIV. Modification of Agreement

Any modification of this Agreement is invalid unless it is in writing and signed by both parties.

XV. Choice of Law

Florida law governs the interpretation of this Agreement as well as any tort or statutory claims arising out of the purchase of Classroom Approved Laptops. Florida law also governs the interpretation of this provision.

XVI. Choice of Forum

The mandatory and exclusive venue for any claims based on this Agreement or arising out of the purchase of Classroom Approved Laptops is Alachua County, Florida.

Executed by the parties as of the date written above.

UF	Apple
____________________	____________________
University of Florida Levin College of Law By: [Name][Title]	Apple, Inc. By: [Name][Title]

Construction Loan Agreement

On this ___ day of ________________, 20___, ______________________________, a ____________________, with a usual place of business at ______________ ______________ (the "Lender") and ________________, a ______________, with a usual place of business at ________________________________ (the "Borrower") enter into this Construction Loan Agreement ("Agreement"). The Lender and the Borrower mutually agree as follows:

SECTION 1. RECITALS

The Borrower has applied to the Lender for a construction loan in the amount of ________________________________ DOLLARS AND 00/100 ($_____ ____.00) (the "Loan"); and the Lender has approved the Borrower's application.

SECTION 2. AGREEMENT

The Lender shall make the Loan to the Borrower upon and subject to all the conditions, terms, covenants and agreements set forth in this Agreement.

SECTION 3. DEFINITIONS

Each reference in this Agreement to the following terms has the following meanings:

Eligible Project Costs:	The costs and expenses listed in the Project Budget (defined below).
Junior Financing:	Collectively, the following loans to the Borrower: $__________ loan from __________, $__________ loan from __________, $__________ loan from __________.
Loan	The loan of $__________.oo to the Borrower by the Lender pursuant to this Agreement, to be used by Borrower for costs of the Project as set forth in the Project Budget.
Loan Documents:	(i) the Note; (ii) the Mortgage; (iii) this Agreement; and (iv) all other documents evidencing or securing the indebtedness evidenced by the Note.
Mortgage:	That Mortgage and Security Agreement of even date from the Borrower to the Lender granting the Lender a mortgage on the Mortgaged Property, recorded with the County Clerk, __________ County Florida.
Mortgaged Property:	The land, together with all the buildings and improvements thereon, together with the Collateral (as defined in the Mortgage), situated at __________, __________ County, Florida, more fully described on Exhibit A.
Note:	The Promissory Note of even date made by the Borrower in the amount of __________ Thousand Dollars ($__________), payable to the order of the Lender.
Permitted Encumbrances:	Any encumbrances enumerated on the mortgagee title insurance policy issued to the Lender for the Loan.
Plans and specifications:	The Plans and Specifications describing the construction of the Project, more fully described on Exhibit B.
Project:	The construction of ____ units of rental housing on the Mortgaged Property.
Project Budget:	The budget for the Project describing in detail the work items included in the Project and the cost of each work item, a copy of which is attached as Exhibit C.
Project Schedule:	The schedule for the construction of the Project set forth in Exhibit D.

SECTION 4. CONDITIONS PRECEDENT

4.1 The obligation of the Lender to make the Loan is subject to the following conditions precedent:

(A) The Borrower shall have and maintain good and marketable title to the Mortgaged Property and the Borrower shall maintain full possession of the Mortgaged Property free and clear of all liens and encumbrances except for the Permitted Encumbrances.

(B) The Borrower shall duly execute or cause to be duly executed by the parties, and have the originals or copies, at Lender's option, of the following documents delivered to the Lender:

(i) The Note;

(ii) The Mortgage;

(iii) This Agreement;

(iv) The following documents as may be required and approved by the Lender: written opinions of the Borrower's counsel as to (1) the existence and authority of the Borrower and due execution and enforceability of the documents to be executed by the Borrower in connection with the Loan, and (2) the compliance of the Project with applicable building, zoning, subdivision, licensing, rent control, historic preservation, environmental, planning land use, and sanitation laws and regulations; and

(v) Such other documentation or due diligence information as may be required by Lender, including, without limitation, a UCC Financing Statement granting to the Lender a security interest in and to all improvements, fixtures and equipment now or hereafter located on or used in connection with the Mortgaged Property and all rents, issues, benefits and profits arising from the foregoing and all fixtures, machinery, equipment, furniture, furnishings, goods, chattel, and other articles of personal property now or at any time attached to or used in any way in connection with the Mortgaged Property or intended for such use, whether or not so attached, and whether not owned or acquired; all cash and non-cash proceeds from the foregoing; and all general intangibles, contract rights and profits and all books of account and records pertaining to, or arising out of the operation of the Mortgaged Property (collectively, the "Personal Property").

4.2 The obligation of the Lender to advance the proceeds under the Loan for construction of the Project is subject to the following conditions precedent:

(A) Inspection of the Mortgaged Property by a representative of the Lender and approval by the Lender of the Plans and Specification for the Project;

(B) Approval by the Lender of the Project Budget, which budget contains detailed breakdowns of the cost of the work by tasks and trades, and the Project Schedule;

(C) Approval by Lender of the Contractor for the Project (the "Contractor") selected by the Borrower.

(D) Execution of a construction contract between the Borrower and the Contractor, satisfactory to the Lender;

(E) Execution of a contract between the Borrower and the architect for the Project (the "Architect"), satisfactory to the Lender;

(F) Approval of the Plans and Specifications for the Project by all local, state, and federal authorities having jurisdiction over the work;

(G) Issuance of a building permit with respect to the Project; and

(H) The certification by the Borrower to the Lender that all representations and warranties contained herein continue to be true in all respects, and there is no Event of Default under this Agreement, the Note, the Mortgage, or any loan document executed in connection with the Junior Financing.

Without at any time waiving any of the Lender's rights, the Lender may make advances without the satisfaction of each and every condition precedent set forth in this Agreement, including, without limitation, in this Section 4.2 and Section 4.3 below, to the Lender's obligation to make any such advance, and the Borrower shall accept such advance as the Lender may elect to make. The making of any advance does not constitute an approval or acceptance by the Lender of any work on the Project previously completed.

4.3 The Lender shall make advances of the first ______________________________ dollars ($______________) of the proceeds of the Loan under the following conditions:

(A) At least ten (10) business days before the date on which an advance is requested to be made, the Borrower shall give notice to the Lender specifying the total advance which will be desired. In the notice, the Borrower shall provide a detailed request describing the completed items of work and shall be accompanied by copies of bills, invoices or other satisfactory documentation of expenses incurred or owing for costs included in the Project Budget in an amount equal to the amount of the requested advance, including, without limitation, receipted bills paid by the Borrower covered by the prior advances. The Borrower shall also provide lien releases or lien bonds in recordable form executed by the Contractor and all subcontractors waiving any and all lien rights which any of them may have with respect to all work performed or materials supplied to date in connection with the Mortgaged Property other than that reflected in the current requests for payment. Upon approval of a requested advance and satisfaction of all conditions set forth below, the Lender shall make the requested advance in the form of a check payable to the Borrower, which check shall be forwarded by the Lender to the Borrower.

(B) The Borrower shall submit requisitions for construction costs on an AIA G702 and/or AIA G703 form. The Lender may require a certification by a construction inspector acceptable to Lender that the construction work is acceptable and consistent with the

Project Budget and the approved Plans and Specifications. The Borrower shall pay the costs incurred by Lender with respect to such construction inspector. Lender may require as a condition of any advance that Borrower submit satisfactory evidence that (i) all funds which have been previously advanced under the Project Budget to the Borrower have been expended in accordance with the Project Budget; and (ii) the unadvanced portion of the Loan together with the unadvanced funds of all other funding sources shown in the Project Budget are sufficient to pay all costs for the completion of the Project in accordance with the approved Plans and Specifications.

(C) Prior to funding of an interim requisition, the Lender may cause the Project to be inspected by a representative of the Lender to verify that the work items described in the request have been actually completed in accordance with the approved Plans and Specifications. The Borrower shall pay the costs incurred by Lender with respect to such construction inspector.

(D) Prior to the funding of the final requisition, the Lender may require a final inspection by a construction professional satisfactory to the Lender confirming that the construction work was performed in a good and workmanlike manner and is consistent with the Project Budget and the approved Plans and Specifications. The Borrower shall pay the costs incurred by Lender with respect to such construction inspector. The final inspection includes verification that (i) the Mortgaged Property is in compliance with all applicable building, zoning and sanitation ordinances, regulations and laws, (ii) all work has been completed in accordance with the approved Plans and Specifications, (iii) all necessary occupancy permits have been obtained, and (iv) all guarantees and warranties are in place.

(E) The Lender shall disburse Loan proceeds only for Eligible Project Costs.

(F) The Borrower shall not make requests for advances until the funds are needed for payment of costs included in the Project Budget and the amount of each request is be limited to the amount needed. The Lender may withhold retainage in the total amount of $________ (ten percent (10%) of the amount of each advance) until final completion of the Project.

(G) The Borrower shall provide to the Lender a mortgagee title insurance policy and/or an endorsement to the Lender's mortgagee title insurance policy at the time of each advance, satisfactory in form and substance to the Lender, re-dating the policy to the date that the then current advance will be made, and increasing the coverage afforded by such policy so that the same shall constitute insurance of the lien of the Mortgage in an amount equal to the aggregate amount advanced under this Agreement as of the date that the then current advance is made available to the Borrower.

(H) By requesting an advance, the Borrower represents and warrants that all representations and warranties contained in this Agreement are true in all respects, and no Event of Default has occurred under this Agreement, the Note, or the Mortgage, or any loan document executed in connection with the Junior Financing.

4.4 The Lender shall advance the remaining ____________________________ dollars ($___________) of the proceeds of the Loan upon the satisfaction of the conditions set forth in section 4.3 (D) above.

SECTION 5. REPRESENTATIONS, WARRANTIES OF THE BORROWER

The Borrower represents and warrants to the Lender that:

5.1 The Borrower is a limited partnership, duly organized and validly existing in accordance with and in good standing under the laws of Georgia.

5.2 The Borrower has the requisite power and authority to own the Project and to carry on business as now being conducted and as contemplated under this Agreement;

5.3 The Borrower has the requisite power to execute and perform this Agreement and has the power to borrow and to execute, deliver and perform under all other Loan Documents;

5.4 The Borrower has good and clear record and marketable title to the Mortgaged Property, subject only to the Permitted Encumbrances and the mortgages granted in connection with the Junior Financing;

5.5 The execution and performance by the Borrower of the terms and provisions of this Agreement and all other Loan Documents have been duly authorized by all requisite action required to be taken by the Borrower, does not violate any provision of law, any order of any court or other agency of government, or any indenture, agreement, or other instrument to which the Borrower is a party, or by which it is bound, and is not in conflict with, result in a breach of or constitute (with due notice or lapse of time, or both) a default under any such indenture, agreement, or other instrument, or result in the creation or imposition of any lien, charge, or encumbrance of any nature whatsoever upon any of the property or assets of the Borrower, other than the Mortgage and the Permitted Encumbrances;

5.6 The Financial data, reports and other information furnished to Lender by the Borrower are accurate and complete and fairly present the financial position of the Borrower.

5.7 There has been no adverse change in the condition, financial or otherwise, of the Borrower since the date of the most recent financial statement referred in Section 5.6;

5.8 There is no action, suit or proceeding at law or in equity or by or before any governmental instrumentality or other agency now pending or, to the knowledge of the Borrower, threatened against or affecting the Borrower which, if adversely determined, would have anare no adverse effect on the business, operations, properties (including the Mortgaged Property), assets or condition, financial or otherwise of the Borrower;

5.9 The Borrower has obtained or will cause to be obtained all necessary governmental permits for the Project; and the dwellings on the Mortgaged Property after completion of the Project will comply with all applicable building, zoning, subdivision, landuse, health, historic preservation, licensing, rent control, planning, sanitation, architectural access, lead paint removal, and all applicable environmental protection ordinances, regulations or laws;

5.10 There are no defaults or sets of facts which, with the passage of time or otherwise, would constitute a default (i) under any agreements by and between the Borrower and the lenders providing the Junior Financing, (ii) under this Agreement or any other Loan Documents, (iii) or under the organizational documents of the Borrower; and

5.11 The proceeds of the Loan and the Junior Financing, and any other sources of funds disclosed by the Borrower to the Lender, provide sufficient funds to complete and operate the Project in accordance with the provisions and requirements of this Agreement.

Each of the foregoing representations, warranties, and covenants survives the making of the Loan and any advance of funds pursuant to this Agreement.

SECTION 6. BORROWER'S COVENANTS

During the term of the Loan, the Borrower shall comply with all of the terms and conditions of the Loan Documents, and the Borrower shall:

6.1 Commence and diligently and continuously continue construction of the Project in a timely manner and in accordance with the Project Schedule and the Project Budget, and substantially in accordance with the Plans and Specifications.

6.2 Construct the Project in compliance with all applicable laws, regulations, codes and ordinances. The Borrower shall notify the Lender when the

Project is complete; and provide to the Lender certifications or documentation as necessary to establish the following:

(i) certificates of occupancy have been issued for all units in the Project;

(ii) a certificate has been executed by the architect for the Project stating that the Mortgaged Property complies with all applicable laws, codes, ordinances, and regulations; and

(iii) all funds advanced under this Agreement were expended for Eligible Project Costs.

6.3 Operate the Project in accordance with provisions of the Mortgage and the other Loan Documents.

6.4 Continuously comply with (i) all applicable building, fire, licensing, health, sanitation, historic preservation, environmental protection, rent control, landuse, subdivision and zoning ordinances, and regulations promulgated by any national, state, or local governmental body, agency or division having jurisdiction over the Mortgaged Property, (ii) the organizational documents of the Borrower, and (iii) all restrictions or other encumbrances affecting title to the Mortgaged Property. The Borrower shall comply with the applicable requirements of the national and local boards of the fire underwriters and furnish to the Lender such evidence of compliance as the Lender may require.

6.5 Keep proper and separate books of account and make, or cause to be made, full and true entries of all dealings and transactions of every kind relating to the Mortgaged Property, which books and records are to be open to inspection by the Lender, its agents, and representatives at the Mortgaged Property or at the Borrower's principal office within the State of Georgia.

6.6 Furnish the Lender with such reports, financial statements, records, and other information relating to the financial condition or operations of the Borrower and the construction and operation of the Project, as the Lender may require, including, but not limited to, (i) annual audited financial statements of the Borrower (to be delivered to the Lender within one hundred twenty (120) days of the end of Borrower's fiscal year), and (ii) such other reports to show that the Project is being built and operated consistently with this Agreement, the organizational documents of the Borrower, and the other Loan Documents.

6.7 Perform all its obligations and agreements under the loan documents executed in connection with the Junior Financing, the organizational documents of the Borrower, and any other agreements or instruments to which the Borrower is a party, and which relate to the Loan or to the Project. The Borrower shall give notice to the Lender of any notices received by it from any lender providing the Junior Financing relative to any default or delinquency under the Junior Financing. The Borrower shall not increase the amount of, amend, terminate, renew, extend, or refinance the Junior Financing, without the prior written consent of the Lender.

6.8 Promptly before they expire, renew all licenses or other permits required for operation of the Project, and provide copies of the same to the Lender no later than ten (10) days after receipt.

6.9 Use Loan proceeds solely for Eligible Project Costs included and ensure that the proceeds of the Loan are not to be re-loaned or assigned to any party and are not to be used for any purpose prohibited by the Loan Documents.

6.10 Upon request and subject to zoning or other land use regulation, permit a sign to be erected on the Mortgaged Property at a location selected by the Lender indicating that the Mortgaged Property is being financed in part by the Lender.

6.11 Not amend or modify the Borrower's articles of organization or bylaws without the Lender's prior written consent.

6.12 Until completion of the Project, cause to be maintained in full force and effect a policy or policies of builder's risk completed value insurance with fire, earthquake and extended coverage, all in such form and in such amounts as the Lender from time to time requires.

SECTION 7. EVENTS OF DEFAULT

The occurrence of any one or more of the following events constitutes an "Event of Default" under the terms of this Agreement:

7.1 The Borrower assigns this Agreement or any money advanced under this Agreement or any interest in this Agreement or if any interest of the Borrower in the Mortgaged Property is terminated, sold, conveyed, or otherwise transferred, without the prior written consent of the Lender (excluding the replacement of equipment by the Borrower).

7.2 Any representation or warranty made in this Agreement or in any report, certificate, financial statement, or other instrument furnished in connection with this Agreement, or the Loan proves to be false in any respect as of the date given.

7.3 The Borrower fails to pay the principal of, or fees or interest on, the Note or any other indebtedness of the Borrower under the Loan Documents after the same is due and payable and such failure continues beyond the date which is ten (10) days after written demand is made by the Lender.

7.4 The Borrower defaults in the due observance or performance of any other covenant, condition, or agreement to be observed or performed by the Borrower pursuant to the terms of any of the Loan Documents and such default remains uncured thirty (30) days after written notice is given by the Lender to the Borrower; provided, however, that if the curing of such default cannot reasonably be accomplished with due diligence within said period of thirty (30) days, then the Borrower has such additional reasonable period of time to cure such default as may be necessary, not to exceed an additional ninety (90) days, so long as: (i) the Borrower has commenced to cure such default within said thirty (30) day period and diligently prosecutes such cure to completion, and (ii) the Lender does not deem the Mortgaged Property jeopardized by such further delay.

7.5 The Borrower (i) applies for or consents to the appointment of a receiver, trustee or liquidator of the Mortgaged Property, (ii) admits in writing its inability to pay its debts as they mature, (iii) makes a general assignment for the benefit of creditors, or (iv) is adjudicated a bankrupt or insolvent (however such insolvency may be evidenced).

7.6 Any proceeding involving the Borrower is commenced by or against the Borrower under any bankruptcy or reorganization arrangement, probate, insolvency, readjustment of debt, dissolution, or liquidation law of the United States, or any state, but if such proceedings are instituted, no Event of Default occurs under this Agreement unless the Borrower either approves, consents to, or acquiesces in such proceedings, or such proceedings are not dismissed no later than sixty (60) days after they were commenced.

7.7 An order, judgment, or decree is entered, without the application, approval, or consent of the Borrower, by any court of competent jurisdiction approving a petition seeking reorganization or approving the appointment of a receiver, trustee, or liquidator of the Borrower, or all or a substantial part of its assets, and such order, judgment, or decree continues unstayed and in effect for a period of sixty (60) days after it was entered.

7.8 Any change in the legal form of, or the beneficial interest in the Borrower or either of its participants, or the termination or dissolution of the Borrower.

7.9 Any judgment, warrant, writ of attachment, or any similar process (in an amount exceeding $10,000, or, if more than one action, when added together all such actions exceed $10,000) is issued or filed against the Borrower or against property or assets of the same, and is not vacated, bonded or stayed, or satisfied within sixty (60) days.

7.10 Failure on the part of the Borrower, continuing beyond any applicable grace or cure period, in the due observance or performance of any other covenant, condition, or agreement to be observed or performed pursuant to the loan documents executed in connection with the Junior Financing, or any other mortgage note or any documents or instruments now or hereafter existing entered into by the Borrower and secured by the Mortgaged Property.

SECTION 8. RIGHTS ON DEFAULT

Upon the occurrence of any one or more of the Events of Default enumerated in the foregoing Section 7, and at any time thereafter, then:

8.1 The Lender may declare all indebtedness due under the Note and any and all other indebtedness of the Borrower to the Lender due under the other Loan Documents or otherwise to be due and payable, whether or not the indebtedness evidenced by the Note or the other Loan Documents is otherwise due and payable and whether or not the Lender has initiated any foreclosure or other action for the enforcement pursuant to the provisions of the Loan Documents, whereupon all indebtedness due under the Note and the other Loan Documents and any other such indebtedness becomes forthwith due and payable, both as to principal and interest, without presentment, demand, protest, or notice of any kind, all of which are expressly waived by the Borrower.

8.2 For the purposes of carrying out the provisions and exercising the rights, powers, and privileges granted by this Section 8, the Borrower hereby irrevocably constitutes and appoints the Lender its true and lawful attorneyinfact with full power of substitution, to execute, acknowledge and deliver any instruments and to perform any acts which are referred to in this Section 8, in the name and on behalf of the Borrower. The power vested in said attorneyinfact is coupled with an interest and irrevocable.

8.3 Upon the occurrence of any of said Events of Default, the Lender may exercise the rights, powers, and privileges provided in this Section 8 and all other remedies available to the Lender under this Agreement or under any of the other Loan Documents or at law or in equity, including but not limited to the commencement of foreclosure proceedings under the Mortgage, the right to cure Borrower's defaults as more fully set forth in the Mortgage or the commencement of an action seeking specific performance under any Loan Documents, whether or not the indebtedness evidenced and secured by the Loan Documents or otherwise is due and payable, and whether or not the Lender has instituted any foreclosure proceedings or other action for the enforcement of its rights under any of the Loan Documents. Failure of the

Lender to exercise any rights or remedies at any time does not constitute a waiver of any of the rights or remedies of the Lender.

SECTION 9. MISCELLANEOUS

9.1 The Borrower shall not assign or attempt to assign directly or indirectly, any of its rights under this Agreement or under any instrument referred to in this Agreement without the prior written consent of the Lender in each instance. Any assignee or purported assignee is bound by all the terms of the assigned documents.

9.2 The Borrower and the Lender shall provide any notice, request, instruction, or other document to be given under this Agreement to each other in writing and delivered personally, or sent by certified or registered mail, postage prepaid, to the addresses set forth in below. Either party may change the address(es) to which notices are to be sent to such party by giving written notice of such change of address to the other party in the manner provided for giving notice. Any such notice, request, instruction, or other document is conclusively deemed to have been received and be effective on the day on which personally delivered or, if sent by certified or registered mail, on the day on which mailed. Lender shall use reasonable efforts to send courtesy copies of all notices sent to Borrower to Borrower's counsel at the address set forth below, provided that any failure to send such a courtesy copy shall not affect the validity of any notice:

If to Borrower:

____

____

____

____

Attention: ____________________

With a courtesy copy to:

____

____

____

____

Attention: ________________

If to Lender:

____

____

____

____

Attention: ________________

With a courtesy copy to:

____

____

____

____

Attention: ________________

9.3 The Loan Documents are governed by the laws of the State of Georgia. Georgia choice of law principles apply to the interpretation of this provision.

9.4 No modification or waiver of any provision of the Loan Documents, nor consent to any departure by the Borrower from the Loan Documents is effective unless the same is in writing, and then such waiver or consent is effective only in the specific instance and for the purpose for which given. No failure or delay on the part of the Lender in exercising any right, power, or privilege under this Agreement or under the Note or the Loan Documents operates as a waiver under such documents, nor does single or partial exercise of such waiver preclude any other or further exercise or the exercise of any other right, power, or privilege.

9.5 This Agreement and all covenants, agreements, representations and warranties made in this Agreement survive the making by the Lender of the Loan and the execution and delivery to the Lender of the Loan Documents, and the completion of the Project, and continue in full force and effect so long as the Note is outstanding and unpaid. This Agreement inures to the benefit of and is binding on the successors and assigns of the Lender and the permitted successors and assigns of the Borrower.

9.6 All Exhibits referred to in this Agreement are by such references fully incorporated into this Agreement.

The Lender and the Borrower have each duly executed, or caused to be duly executed, this Agreement in the name and behalf of each of them (acting by their respective officers or appropriate legal representatives, as the case may be, duly authorized) as of the day and year first above written.

BORROWER:

____

By: __________________________

By: __________________________
Name:
Title:

LENDER: ______________________

By: __________________________
Name:
Title:

Exhibit A: Property Description
Exhibit B: Plans and Specifications
Exhibit C: Project Budget
Exhibit D: Project Schedule

CONSTRUCTION LOAN AGREEMENT
for Salvatori Project

On this ___ day of ________________, 20_, Archer Bank, a ________________ _________, with a usual place of business at 4 Sunrise Terrace, Micanopy, Florida (the "Lender") and Alberto Salvatori, an individual with a ~~usual place of business~~ residence at 333 South Street, Micanopy, Florida (the "Borrower") enter into this Construction Loan Agreement ("Agreement"). The Lender and the Borrower mutually agree as follows:

SECTION 1. RECITALS

The Borrower has applied to the Lender for a construction loan in the amount of ONE HUNDRED FIFTY THOUSAND DOLLARS AND 00/100 ($150,000.00) (the "Loan"); and the Lender has approved the Borrower's application.

SECTION 2. AGREEMENT

The Lender shall make the Loan to the Borrower upon and subject to all the conditions, terms, covenants, and agreements set forth in this Agreement.

SECTION 3. DEFINITIONS

Each reference in this Agreement to the following terms has the following meanings:

Eligible Project Costs:	The costs and expenses listed in the Project Budget (defined below), including the cost to acquire the Mortgaged Property.
~~Junior Financing:~~	~~Collectively, the following loans to the Borrower: $__________ loan from __________, $__________ loan from __________, $__________ loan from __________.~~
Loan	The loan of $150,000.00 to the Borrower by the Lender pursuant to this Agreement, to be used by Borrower for costs of the Project as set forth in the Project Budget.
Loan Documents:	(i) the Note; (ii) the Mortgage; (iii) this Agreement; and (iv) all other documents evidencing or securing the indebtedness evidenced by the Note.
Mortgage:	That Mortgage and Security Agreement of even date from the Borrower to the Lender granting the Lender a mortgage on the Mortgaged Property, recorded with the County Clerk, Marion County Florida.
Mortgaged Property:	The land, together with all the buildings and improvements thereon, together with the Collateral (as defined in the Mortgage), situated at 7 Palm Court, Macintosh, Marion County, Florida, more fully described on Exhibit A.
Note:	The Promissory Note of even date made by the Borrower in the amount of One Hundred Fifty Thousand Dollars ($150,000.00), payable to the order of the Lender.
Permitted Encumbrances:	Any encumbrances enumerated on the mortgagee title insurance policy issued to the Lender for the Loan.
Plans and specifications:	The Plans and Specifications describing the construction of the Project, more fully described on Exhibit B.
Project:	The construction of ~~____ units of rental housing~~ one (1) single family home on the Mortgaged Property.
Project Budget:	The budget for the Project describing in detail the work items included in the Project and the cost of each work item, a copy of which is attached as Exhibit C.

Project Schedule:	The schedule for the construction of the Project set forth in Exhibit D.

SECTION 4. CONDITIONS PRECEDENT

4.1 The obligation of the Lender to make the Loan is subject to the following conditions precedent:

(A) The Borrower shall have and maintain good and marketable title to the Mortgaged Property and the Borrower shall maintain full possession of the Mortgaged Property free and clear of all liens and encumbrances except for the Permitted Encumbrances.

(B) The Borrower shall duly execute or cause to be duly executed by the parties, and have the originals or copies, at Lender's option, of the following documents delivered to the Lender:

(i) The Note;
(ii) The Mortgage;
(iii) This Agreement;
(iv) The following documents as may be required and approved by the Lender: written opinions of the Borrower's counsel as to (1) the existence and authority of the Borrower and due execution and enforceability of the documents to be executed by the Borrower in connection with the Loan, and (2) the compliance of the Project with applicable building, zoning, subdivision, licensing, rent control, historic preservation, environmental, planning land use, and sanitation laws and regulations; and
(v) Such other documentation or due diligence information as may be required by Lender, including, without limitation, a UCC Financing Statement granting to the Lender a security interest in and to all improvements, fixtures, and equipment now or hereafter located on or used in connection with the Mortgaged Property and all rents, issues, benefits, and

profits arising from the foregoing and all fixtures, machinery, equipment, furniture, furnishings, goods, chattel, and other articles of personal property now or at any time attached to or used in any way in connection with the Mortgaged Property or intended for such use, whether or not so attached, and whether or not owned or acquired; all cash and non-cash proceeds from the foregoing; and all general intangibles, contract rights and profits, and all books of account and records pertaining to, or arising out of the operation of the Mortgaged Property (collectively, the "Personal Property").

4.2 The obligation of the Lender to advance the proceeds under the Loan for construction of the Project is subject to the following conditions precedent:

(A) Inspection of the Mortgaged Property by a representative of the Lender and approval by the Lender of the Plans and Specification for the Project;

(B) Approval by the Lender of the Project Budget, which budget contains detailed breakdowns of the cost of the work by tasks and trades, and the Project Schedule;

~~(C) Approval by Lender of the Contractor for the Project (the "Contractor") selected by the Borrower.~~

(~~D~~C) Execution of a construction contract between the Borrower and Homes, Inc. (the "Contractor"), satisfactory to the Lender;

~~(E) Execution of a contract between the Borrower and the architect for the Project (the "Architect"), satisfactory to the Lender;~~

(~~F~~D) Approval of the Plans and Specifications for the Project by all local, state, and federal authorities having jurisdiction over the work;

(~~G~~E) Issuance of a building permit with respect to the Project; and

(~~H~~F) The certification by the Borrower to the Lender that all representations and warranties contained herein continue to be true in all respects, and there is no Event of Default under this Agreement, the Note, the Mortgage~~, or any loan document executed in connection with the Junior Financing~~.

Without at any time waiving any of the Lender's rights, the Lender may make advances without the satisfaction of each and every condition precedent set forth in this Agreement, including, without limitation, in this Section 4.2 and Section 4.3 below, to the Lender's obligation to make any such advance, and the Borrower shall accept such advance as the Lender may elect to make. The making of any advance does not constitute an approval or acceptance by the Lender of any work on the Project previously completed.

4.3 The Lender shall make advances of the first ______________________ dollars ($____________) of the proceeds of the Loan under the following conditions:

(A) At least ten (10) business days before the date on which an advance is requested to be made, the Borrower shall give notice to the Lender specifying the total advance which will be desired. In the notice, the Borrower shall provide a detailed request describing the completed items of work and shall be accompanied by copies of bills, invoices, or other satisfactory documentation of expenses incurred or owing for costs included in the Project Budget in an amount equal to the amount of the requested advance, including, without limitation, receipted bills paid by the Borrower covered by the prior advances. The Borrower shall also provide lien releases or lien bonds in recordable form executed by the Contractor and all subcontractors waiving any and all lien rights which any of them may have with respect to all work performed or materials supplied to date in connection with the Mortgaged Property other than that reflected in the current requests for payment. Upon approval of a requested advance and satisfaction of all conditions set forth below, the Lender shall make the requested advance in the form of a check payable to the

Borrower, which check shall be forwarded by the Lender to the Borrower.

(B) The Borrower shall submit requisitions for construction costs on an AIA G702 and/or AIA G703 form. The Lender may require a certification by a construction inspector acceptable to Lender that the construction work is acceptable and consistent with the Project Budget and the approved Plans and Specifications. The Borrower shall pay the costs incurred by Lender with respect to such construction inspector. Lender may require as a condition of any advance that Borrower submit satisfactory evidence that (i) all funds which have been previously advanced under the Project Budget to the Borrower have been expended in accordance with the Project Budget and (ii) the unadvanced portion of the Loan together with the unadvanced funds of all other funding sources shown in the Project Budget are sufficient to pay all costs for the completion of the Project in accordance with the approved Plans and Specifications.

(C) Prior to the funding of an interim requisition, the Lender may cause the Project to be inspected by a representative of the Lender to verify that the work items described in the request have been actually completed in accordance with the approved Plans and Specifications. The Borrower shall pay the costs incurred by Lender with respect to such construction inspector.

(D) Prior to the funding of the final requisition, the Lender may require a final inspection by a construction professional satisfactory to the Lender confirming that the construction work was performed in a good and workmanlike manner and is consistent with the Project Budget and the approved Plans and Specifications. The Borrower shall pay the costs incurred by Lender with respect to such construction inspector. The final inspection includes verification that (i) the Mortgaged Property is in compliance with all applicable building, zoning and sanitation ordinances, regulations and laws, (ii) all work has been completed in accordance with the approved Plans and Specifications, (iii) all necessary occupancy permits have been obtained, and (iv) all guarantees and warranties are in place.

(E) The Lender shall disburse Loan proceeds only for Eligible Project Costs.

(F) The Borrower shall not make requests for advances until the funds are needed for payment of costs included in the Project Budget and the amount of each request is to be limited to the amount needed. ~~The Lender may withhold retainage in the total amount of $__________ (ten percent (10%) of the amount of each advance) until final completion of the Project.~~

(G) The Borrower shall provide to the Lender a mortgagee title insurance policy and/or an endorsement to the Lender's mortgagee title insurance policy at the time of each advance, satisfactory in form and substance to the Lender, re-dating the policy to the date that the then current advance will be made, and increasing the coverage afforded by such policy so that the same shall constitute insurance of the lien of the Mortgage in an amount equal to the aggregate amount advanced under this Agreement as of the date that the then current advance is made available to the Borrower.

(H) By requesting an advance, the Borrower represents and warrants that all representations and warranties contained in this Agreement are true in all respects, and no Event of Default has occurred under this Agreement, the Note, or the Mortgage~~, or any loan document executed in connection with the Junior Financing~~.

4.4 The Lender shall advance the remaining ______________________________ dollars ($________) of the proceeds of the Loan upon the satisfaction of the conditions set forth in section 4.3 (D) above.

SECTION 5. REPRESENTATIONS, WARRANTIES OF THE BORROWER

The Borrower represents and warrants to the Lender that:

5.1 ~~The Borrower is a limited partnership, duly organized and validly existing in accordance with and in good standing under the laws of Georgia.~~ Intentionally omitted.

5.2 The Borrower has the requisite power and authority to own the Project and to carry on business as now being conducted and as contemplated under this Agreement;

5.3 The Borrower has the requisite power to execute and perform this Agreement and has the power to borrow and to execute, deliver, and perform under all other Loan Documents;

5.4 The Borrower has good and clear record and marketable title to the Mortgaged Property, subject only to the Permitted Encumbrances ~~and the mortgages granted in connection with the Junior Financing~~;

5.5 The execution and performance by the Borrower of the terms and provisions of this Agreement and all other Loan Documents ~~have been duly authorized by all requisite action required to be taken by the Borrower~~, does not violate any provision of law, any order of any court or other agency of government, or any indenture, agreement, or other instrument to which the Borrower is a party or by which it is bound, and is not in conflict with, result in a breach of, or constitute (with due notice or lapse of time or both) a default under any such indenture, agreement or other instrument, or result in the creation or imposition of any lien, charge, or encumbrance of any nature whatsoever upon any of the property or assets of the Borrower, other than the Mortgage and the Permitted Encumbrances;

5.6 The Financial data, reports, and other information furnished to Lender by the Borrower are accurate and complete and fairly present the financial position of the Borrower.

5.7 There has been no adverse change in the condition, financial or otherwise, of the Borrower since the date of the most recent financial statement referred in Section 5.6;

5.8 There is no action, suit, or proceeding at law or in equity or by or before any governmental instrumentality or other agency now pending or, to the knowledge of the Borrower, threatened against or affecting the Borrower which, if adversely determined, would have an adverse effect on the business, operations, properties (including the Mortgaged Property), assets, or condition, financial or otherwise of the Borrower;

5.9 The Borrower has obtained or will cause to be obtained all necessary governmental permits for the Project; and the dwellings on the Mortgaged Property after completion of the Project will comply with all applicable building, zoning, subdivision, landuse, health, historic preservation, licensing, rent control, planning, sanitation, architectural access, lead paint removal, and all applicable environmental protection ordinances, regulations, or laws;

5.10 There are no defaults or sets of facts which, with the passage of time or otherwise, would constitute a default ~~(i) under any agreements by and between the Borrower and the lenders providing the Junior Financing, (ii)~~ under this Agreement or any other Loan Documents~~, (iii) or under the organizational documents of the Borrower~~; and

5.11The proceeds of the Loan ~~and the Junior Financing~~, and any other sources of funds disclosed by the Borrower to the Lender, provide sufficient funds to complete and operate the Project in accordance with the provisions and requirements of this Agreement.

Each of the foregoing representations, warranties, and covenants survives the making of the Loan and any advance of funds pursuant to this Agreement.

SECTION 6. BORROWER'S COVENANTS

During the term of the Loan, the Borrower shall comply with all of the terms and conditions of the Loan Documents, and the Borrower shall:

6.1 Commence and diligently and continuously continue construction of the Project in a timely manner and in accordance with the Project Schedule and the Project Budget, and substantially in accordance with the Plans and Specifications.

6.2 Construct the Project in compliance with all applicable laws, regulations, codes and ordinances. The Borrower shall notify the Lender when the Project is complete; and provide to the Lender certifications or documentation as necessary to establish the following:

- (i) certificates of occupancy have been issued for all units in the Project;
- (ii) a certificate has been executed by the ~~architect~~ Contractor for the Project stating that the Mortgaged Property complies with all applicable laws, codes, ordinances, and regulations; and
- (iii) all funds advanced under this Agreement were expended for Eligible Project Costs.

~~6.3 Operate the Project in accordance with provisions of the Mortgage and the other Loan Documents.~~

6.~~4~~3 Continuously comply with (i) all applicable building, fire, licensing, health, sanitation, historic preservation, environmental protection, rent control, landuse, subdivision and zoning ordinances and regulations promulgated by any national, state or local governmental body, agency, or division having jurisdiction over the Mortgaged Property, ~~(ii) the organizational documents of the Borrower~~, and (~~i~~ii) all restrictions or other encumbrances affecting title to the Mortgaged Property. The Borrower shall comply with the applicable requirements of the national and local boards of the fire underwriters and furnish to the Lender such evidence of compliance as the Lender may require.

6.~~5~~4 Keep proper and separate books of account and make, or cause to be made, full and true entries of all dealings and transactions of every kind relating to the Mortgaged Property, which books and records are to be open to inspection by the Lender, its agents and representatives at the Mortgaged Property or at the Borrower's principal office within the State of ~~Georgia~~ Florida.

6.~~6~~5 Furnish the Lender with such reports, financial statements, records, and other information relating to the financial condition or operations of the Borrower and the construction and operation of the Project, as the Lender may require, including, but not limited to, (i) annual audited financial statements [ask client if these will be required] of the Borrower (to be delivered to the Lender within one hundred twenty (120) days of the end of Borrower's fiscal year), and (ii) such other reports to show that the Project is being built ~~and operated~~ consistently with this Agreement, ~~the organizational documents of the Borrower,~~ and the other Loan Documents.

6.~~7~~6 Perform all its obligations and agreements under ~~the loan documents executed in connection with the Junior Financing, the organizational documents of the Borrower, and~~ any ~~other~~ agreements or instruments to which the Borrower is a party, and which relate to the Loan or to the Project. ~~The Borrower shall give notice to the Lender of any notices received by it from any lender providing the Junior Financing relative to any default or delinquency under the Junior Financing. The Borrower shall not increase the amount of, amend, terminate, renew, extend or refinance the Junior Financing, without the prior written consent of the Lender.~~

6.~~8~~7 Indemnify, exonerate and hold harmless the Lender from any and all liability, loss, cost, damage, or expense in connection with the Loan or the Loan Documents, including attorney's fees, except to the extent of Lender's gross negligence or willful misconduct.

6.~~9~~8 Promptly before they expire, renew all licenses or other permits required for operation of the Project, and provide copies of the same to the Lender no later than ten (10) days after receipt.

~~6.10 From and after completion of the Project, provide and operate __________ (___) rental housing units on the Mortgaged Property.~~

6.~~11~~9 Use Loan proceeds solely for Eligible Project Costs included and ensure that the proceeds of the Loan are not to be re-loaned or assigned to any party and are not used for any purpose prohibited by the Loan Documents.

6.~~12~~10 Upon request and subject to zoning or other land use regulation, permit a sign to be erected on the Mortgaged Property at a location selected by the Lender indicating that the Mortgaged Property is being financed in part by the Lender.

~~6.13 Not amend or modify the Borrower's articles of organization or bylaws without the Lender's prior written consent.~~

6.~~14~~11 Until completion of the Project, cause to be maintained in full force and effect a policy or policies of builder's risk completed value insurance with fire, earthquake, and extended coverage, all in such form and in such amounts as the Lender from time to time requires.

SECTION 7. EVENTS OF DEFAULT

The occurrence of any one or more of the following events constitutes an "Event of Default" under the terms of this Agreement:

7.1 The Borrower assigns this Agreement or any money advanced under this Agreement or any interest in this Agreement or if any interest of the Borrower in the Mortgaged Property is terminated, sold, conveyed, or otherwise transferred, without the prior written consent of the Lender (excluding the replacement of equipment by the Borrower).

7.2 Any representation or warranty made in this Agreement or in any report, certificate, financial statement, or other instrument furnished in connection with this Agreement or the Loan proves to be false in any respect as of the date given.

7.3 The Borrower fails to pay the principal of, or fees or interest on, the Note or any other indebtedness of the Borrower under the Loan Documents after the same is due and payable and such failure continues beyond the date which is ten (10) days after written demand is made by the Lender.

7.4 The Borrower defaults in the due observance or performance of any other covenant, condition or agreement to be observed or performed by the

Borrower pursuant to the terms of any of the Loan Documents and such default remains uncured thirty (30) days after written notice is given by the Lender to the Borrower; provided, however, that if the curing of such default cannot reasonably be accomplished with due diligence within said period of thirty (30) days, then the Borrower has such additional reasonable period of time to cure such default as may be necessary, not to exceed an additional ninety (90) days, so long as: (i) the Borrower has commenced to cure such default within said thirty (30) day period and diligently prosecutes such cure to completion and (ii) the Lender does not deem the Mortgaged Property jeopardized by such further delay.

7.5 The Borrower (i) applies for or consents to the appointment of a receiver, trustee, or liquidator of the Mortgaged Property, (ii) admits in writing its inability to pay its debts as they mature, (iii) makes a general assignment for the benefit of creditors, or (iv) is adjudicated a bankrupt or insolvent (however such insolvency may be evidenced).

7.6 Any proceeding involving the Borrower is commenced by or against the Borrower under any bankruptcy or reorganization arrangement, probate, insolvency, readjustment of debt, dissolution or liquidation law of the United States, or any state, but if such proceedings are instituted, no Event of Default occurs under this Agreement unless the Borrower either approves, consents to, or acquiesces in such proceedings, or such proceedings are not dismissed no later than sixty (60) days after they were commenced.

7.7 An order, judgment or decree is entered, without the application, approval, or consent of the Borrower, by any court of competent jurisdiction approving a petition seeking reorganization or approving the appointment of a receiver, trustee or liquidator of the Borrower or all or a substantial part of its assets, and such order, judgment or decree continues unstayed and in effect for a period of sixty (60) days after it was entered.

7.8 ~~Any change in the legal form of, or the beneficial interest in the Borrower or either of its participants, or the termination or dissolution of the Borrower.~~ Intentionally omitted.

7.9 Any judgment, warrant, writ of attachment, or any similar process (in an amount exceeding $10,000, or, if more than one action, when added together all such actions exceed $10,000) is issued or filed against the Borrower or against property or assets of the same, and is not vacated, bonded, or stayed or satisfied within sixty (60) days.

7.10 Failure on the part of the Borrower, continuing beyond any applicable grace or cure period, in the due observance or performance of any other covenant, condition, or agreement to be observed or performed pursuant to ~~the loan documents executed in connection with the Junior Financing, or~~ any ~~other~~ mortgage note or any documents or instruments now or hereafter existing entered into by the Borrower and secured by the Mortgaged Property.

SECTION 8. RIGHTS ON DEFAULT

Upon the occurrence of any one or more of the Events of Default enumerated in the foregoing Section 7, and at any time thereafter, then:

8.1 The Lender may declare all indebtedness due under the Note and any and all other indebtedness of the Borrower to the Lender due under the other Loan Documents or otherwise to be due and payable, whether or not the indebtedness evidenced by the Note or the other Loan Documents is otherwise due and payable and whether or not the Lender has initiated any foreclosure or other action for the enforcement pursuant to the provisions of the Loan Documents, whereupon all indebtedness due under the Note and the other Loan Documents and any other such indebtedness becomes forthwith due and payable, both as to principal and interest, without presentment, demand, protest, or notice of any kind, all of which are expressly waived by the Borrower.

8.2 For the purposes of carrying out the provisions and exercising the rights, powers, and privileges granted by this Section 8, the Borrower hereby irrevocably constitutes and appoints the Lender its true and lawful attorneyinfact with full power of substitution, to execute, acknowledge and deliver any instruments and to perform any acts which are referred to in this Section 8, in the name and on behalf of the Borrower. The power vested in said attorneyinfact is coupled with an interest and irrevocable.

8.3 Upon the occurrence of any of said Events of Default, the Lender may exercise the rights, powers, and privileges provided in this Section 8 and all other remedies available to the Lender under this Agreement or under any of the other Loan Documents or at law or in equity, including but not limited to the commencement of foreclosure proceedings under the Mortgage, the right to cure Borrower's defaults as more fully set forth in the Mortgage, or the commencement of an action seeking specific performance under any Loan Documents, whether or not the indebtedness evidenced and secured by the Loan Documents or otherwise is due and payable, and whether or not the Lender has instituted any foreclosure proceedings or other action for the enforcement of its rights under any of the Loan Documents. Failure of the Lender to exercise any rights or remedies at any time does not constitute a waiver of any of the rights or remedies of the Lender.

SECTION 9. MISCELLANEOUS

9.1 The Borrower shall not assign or attempt to assign directly or indirectly, any of its rights under this Agreement or under any instrument referred to in this Agreement without the prior written consent of the Lender in each instance. Any assignee or purported assignee is bound by all the terms of the assigned documents.

9.2 The Borrower and the Lender shall provide any notice, request, instruction or other document to be given under this Agreement to each other in writing and delivered personally or sent by certified or registered mail, postage prepaid, to the addresses set forth in below. Either party may change the address(es) to which notices are to be sent to such party by giving written notice of such change of address to the other party in the manner provided for giving notice. Any such notice, request, instruction, or other document is conclusively deemed to have been received and be effective on the day on which personally delivered or, if sent by certified or registered mail, on the day on which mailed. Lender shall use reasonable efforts to send courtesy copies of all notices sent to Borrower to Borrower's counsel at the address set forth below, provided that any failure to send such a courtesy copy shall not affect the validity of any notice:

If to Borrower:
Alberto Salvatori
333 South Street
Micanopy, Florida
~~______________________________~~
~~______________________________~~
~~______________________________~~
~~______________________________~~
~~Attention:~~ ~~___________________~~

~~With a courtesy copy to:~~
~~______________________________~~
~~______________________________~~
~~______________________________~~
~~______________________________~~
~~Attention:~~ ~~___________________~~

If to Lender:
Archer Bank
4 Sunrise Terrace
Micanopy, Florida
~~______________________________~~
~~______________________________~~
~~______________________________~~
~~______________________________~~
~~Attention:~~ ~~___________________~~

~~With a courtesy copy to:~~
~~______________________________~~
~~______________________________~~
~~______________________________~~
~~______________________________~~
~~Attention:~~ ~~___________________~~

9.3 The Loan Documents are governed by the laws of the State of ~~Georgia~~ Florida. ~~Georgia~~ Florida choice of law principles apply to the interpretation of this provision.

9.4 No modification or waiver of any provision of the Loan Documents, nor consent to any departure by the Borrower from the Loan Documents is effective unless the same is in writing, and then such waiver or consent is effective only in the specific instance and for the purpose for which given. No failure or delay on the part of the Lender in exercising any right, power, or privilege under this Agreement or under the Note or the Loan Documents operates as a waiver under such documents, nor does single or partial exercise of such waiver preclude any other or further exercise or the exercise of any other right, power, or privilege.

9.5 This Agreement and all covenants, agreements, representations, and warranties made in this Agreement survive the making by the Lender of the Loan and the execution and delivery to the Lender of the Loan Documents, and the completion of the Project, and continue in full force and effect so long as the Note is outstanding and unpaid. This Agreement inures to the benefit of and is binding on the successors and assigns of the Lender and the permitted successors and assigns of the Borrower.

9.6 All Exhibits referred to in this Agreement are by such references fully incorporated into this Agreement.

The Lender and the Borrower have each duly executed, or caused to be duly executed, this Agreement in the name and on behalf of each of them (acting by their respective officers or appropriate legal representatives, as the case may be, duly authorized) as of the day and year first above written.

BORROWER:

____

~~By:~~ ______________________________

~~By:~~ ______________________________
~~Name:~~ Alberto Salvatori
~~Title:~~

LENDER:
Archer Bank

By: ______________________________
Name:
Title:

Exhibit A: Property Description
Exhibit B: Plans and Specifications
Exhibit C: Project Budget
Exhibit D: Project Schedule

CONSTRUCTION LOAN AGREEMENT
Revised to Better Reflect Borrower's Interests

On this ___ day of ________________, 20___, ______________________________, a ____________________, with a usual place of business at _______________ _______________ (the "Lender") and _______________, a _____________, with a usual place of business at ___________________________________(the "Borrower") enter into this Construction Loan Agreement ("Agreement"). The Lender and the Borrower mutually agree as follows:

SECTION 1. RECITALS

The Borrower has applied to the Lender for a construction loan in the amount of ______________________________________ DOLLARS AND 00/100 ($____ _________.00) (the "Loan"); and the Lender has approved the Borrower's application.

SECTION 2. AGREEMENT

The Lender shall make the Loan to the Borrower upon and subject to all the conditions, terms, covenants, and agreements set forth in this Agreement.

SECTION 3. DEFINITIONS

Each reference in this Agreement to the following terms has the following meanings:

Eligible Project Costs:	The costs and expenses listed in the Project Budget (defined below).
Junior Financing:	Collectively, the following loans to the Borrower: $__________ loan from __________, $__________ loan from __________, $__________ loan from __________.
Loan	The loan of $________________.00 to the Borrower by the Lender pursuant to this Agreement, to be used by Borrower for costs of the Project as set forth in the Project Budget.
Loan Documents:	(i) the Note; (ii) the Mortgage; (iii) this Agreement; and (iv) all other documents evidencing or securing the indebtedness evidenced by the Note.
Mortgage:	That Mortgage and Security Agreement of even date from the Borrower to the Lender granting the Lender a mortgage on the Mortgaged Property, recorded with the County Clerk, __________ County Florida.
Mortgaged Property:	The land, together with all the buildings and improvements thereon, together with the Collateral (as defined in the Mortgage), situated at _________, _________ County, Florida, more fully described on Exhibit A.
Note:	The Promissory Note of even date made by the Borrower in the amount of ________________ Thousand Dollars ($____________), payable to the order of the Lender.
Permitted Encumbrances:	Any encumbrances enumerated on the mortgagee title insurance policy issued to the Lender for the Loan.
Plans and specifications:	The Plans and Specifications describing the construction of the Project, more fully described on Exhibit B.
Project:	The construction of ___ units of rental housing on the Mortgaged Property.
Project Budget:	The budget for the Project describing in detail the work items included in the Project and the cost of each work item, a copy of which is attached as Exhibit C.
Project Schedule:	The schedule for the construction of the Project set forth in Exhibit D.

SECTION 4. CONDITIONS PRECEDENT

4.1 The obligation of the Lender to make the Loan is subject to the following conditions precedent:

(A) The Borrower shall have and maintain good and marketable title to the Mortgaged Property and the Borrower shall maintain full possession of the Mortgaged Property free and clear of all liens and encumbrances except for the Permitted Encumbrances.

(B) The Borrower shall duly execute or cause to be duly executed by the parties, and have the originals or copies, at Lender's option, of the following documents delivered to the Lender:

(i) The Note;
(ii) The Mortgage;
(iii) This Agreement;
(iv) The following documents as may be required and approved by the Lender: written opinions of the Borrower's counsel as to (1) the existence and authority of the Borrower and due execution and enforceability of the documents to be executed by the Borrower in connection with the Loan, and (2) the compliance of the Project with applicable building, zoning, subdivision, licensing, rent control, historic preservation, environmental, planning land use, and sanitation laws and regulations; and
(v) Such other documentation or due diligence information as may be required by Lender, including, without limitation, a UCC Financing Statement granting to the Lender a security interest in and to all improvements, fixtures and equipment now or hereafter located on or used in connection with the Mortgaged Property and all rents, issues, benefits and profits arising from the foregoing and all fixtures, machinery, equipment, furniture, furnishings, goods, chattel, and other articles of personal property now or at any time attached to or used in any way in connection with the Mortgaged Property or intended for such use, whether or not so attached, and whether not owned or acquired; all cash and non-cash

proceeds from the foregoing; and all general intangibles, contract rights and profits and all books of account and records pertaining to, or arising out of the operation of the Mortgaged Property (collectively, the "Personal Property").

4.2 The obligation of the Lender to advance the proceeds under the Loan for construction of the Project is subject to the following conditions precedent:

(A) Inspection of the Mortgaged Property by a representative of the Lender and approval by the Lender of the Plans and Specification for the Project;

(B) Approval by the Lender of the Project Budget, which budget contains detailed breakdowns of the cost of the work by tasks and trades, and the Project Schedule;

(C) Approval by Lender of the Contractor for the Project (the "Contractor") selected by the Borrower.

(D) Execution of a construction contract between the Borrower and the Contractor, <u>reasonably</u> satisfactory to the Lender;

(E) Execution of a contract between the Borrower and the architect for the Project (the "Architect"), <u>reasonably</u> satisfactory to the Lender;

(F) Approval of the Plans and Specifications for the Project by all local, state, and federal authorities having jurisdiction over the work;

(G) Issuance of a building permit with respect to the Project; and

(H) The certification by the Borrower to the Lender that all representations and warranties contained herein continue to be true in all <u>material</u> respects, and <u>to the best of the Borrower's knowledge, information and belief</u>, there is no Event of Default under this Agreement, the Note, the Mortgage, or any loan document executed in connection with the Junior Financing.

Without at any time waiving any of the Lender's rights, the Lender may make advances without the satisfaction of each and every condition precedent set forth in this Agreement, including, without limitation, in this Section 4.2 and Section 4.3 below, to the Lender's obligation to make any such advance, and the Borrower shall accept such advance as the Lender may elect to make. The making of any advance does not constitute an approval or acceptance by the Lender of any work on the Project previously completed.

4.3 The Lender shall make advances of the first ______________________________ dollars ($____________) of the proceeds of the Loan under the following conditions:

(A) At least ten (10) business days before the date on which an advance is requested to be made, the Borrower shall give notice to the Lender specifying the total advance which will be desired. In the notice, the Borrower shall provide a detailed request describing the completed items of work and shall be accompanied by copies of bills, invoices, or other reasonably satisfactory documentation of expenses incurred or owing for costs included in the Project Budget in an amount equal to the amount of the requested advance, including, without limitation, receipted bills paid by the Borrower covered by the prior advances. The Borrower shall also provide lien releases or lien bonds in recordable form executed by the Contractor and all subcontractors waiving any and all lien rights which any of them may have with respect to all work performed or materials supplied to date in connection with the Mortgaged Property other than that reflected in the current requests for payment. Upon approval of a requested advance and satisfaction of all conditions set forth below, the Lender shall make the requested advance in the form of a check payable to the Borrower, which check shall be forwarded by the Lender to the Borrower no later than three (3) days after such approval.

(B) The Borrower shall submit requisitions for construction costs on an AIA G702 and/or AIA G703 form. The Lender may require a certification by a construction inspector acceptable to Lender that the construction work is acceptable and consistent with the Project Budget and the approved Plans and Specifications. The Borrower shall pay the reasonable costs incurred by Lender with respect to such construction inspector. Lender may require as a condition of any advance that Borrower submit reasonably satisfactory evidence that (i) all funds which have been previously advanced under the Project Budget to the Borrower have been expended in accordance with the Project Budget and (ii) the unadvanced portion of the Loan together with the unadvanced funds of all other funding sources shown in the Project Budget are sufficient to pay all costs for the completion of the Project in accordance with the approved Plans and Specifications.

(C) Prior to funding of an interim requisition, the Lender may cause the Project to be inspected by a representative of the Lender to verify that the work items described in the request have been actually completed in accordance with the approved Plans and Specifications. The Borrower shall pay the reasonable costs incurred by Lender with respect to such construction inspector.

(D) Prior to the funding of the final requisition, the Lender may require a final inspection by a construction professional satisfactory to the Lender confirming that the construction work was performed in a good and workmanlike manner and is consistent with the Project Budget and the approved Plans and Specifications. The Borrower shall pay the reasonable costs incurred by Lender with respect to such construction inspector. The final inspection includes verification that (i) the Mortgaged Property is in compliance with all applicable building, zoning, and sanitation ordinances, regulations and laws, (ii) all work has been completed in accordance with the approved Plans and Specifications, (iii) all necessary occupancy permits have been obtained, and (iv) all guarantees and warranties are in place.

(E) The Lender shall disburse Loan proceeds only for Eligible Project Costs.

(F) The Borrower shall not make requests for advances until the funds are needed for payment of costs included in the Project Budget and the amount of each request is be limited to the amount needed. The Lender may withhold retainage in the total amount of $_________ (ten percent (10%) of the amount of each advance) until final completion of the Project.

(G) The Borrower shall provide to the Lender a mortgagee title insurance policy and/or an endorsement to the Lender's mortgagee title insurance policy at the time of each advance, reasonably satisfactory in form and substance to the Lender, re-dating the policy to the date that the then current advance will be made, and increasing the coverage afforded by such policy so that the same shall constitute insurance of the lien of the Mortgage in an amount equal to the aggregate amount advanced under this Agreement as of the date that the then current advance is made available to the Borrower.

(H) By requesting an advance, the Borrower represents and warrants that all representations and warranties contained in this Agreement are true in all material respects, and to the best of Borrower's knowledge, information and belief, no Event of Default has occurred under this Agreement, the Note or the Mortgage, or any loan document executed in connection with the Junior Financing.

4.4 The Lender shall advance the remaining _________________________ dollars ($___________) of the proceeds of the Loan upon the satisfaction of the conditions set forth in section 4.3 (D) above.

SECTION 5. REPRESENTATIONS, WARRANTIES OF THE BORROWER

The Borrower represents and warrants to the Lender that:

5.1 The Borrower is a limited partnership, duly organized and validly existing in accordance with and in good standing under the laws of Georgia.

5.2 The Borrower has the requisite power and authority to own the Project and to carry on business as now being conducted and as contemplated under this Agreement;

5.3 The Borrower has the requisite power to execute and perform this Agreement and has the power to borrow and to execute, deliver and perform under all other Loan Documents;

5.4 The Borrower has good and clear record and marketable title to the Mortgaged Property, subject only to the Permitted Encumbrances and the mortgages granted in connection with the Junior Financing;

5.5 The execution and performance by the Borrower of the terms and provisions of this Agreement and all other Loan Documents have been duly authorized by all requisite action required to be taken by the Borrower, to the best of Borrower's knowledge, does not violate any provision of law, any order of any court or other agency of government, or any indenture, agreement, or other instrument to which the Borrower is a party or by which it is bound, and is not in conflict with, result in a breach of or constitute (with due notice or lapse of time or both) a default under any such indenture, agreement, or other instrument, or result in the creation or imposition of any lien, charge, or encumbrance of any nature whatsoever upon any of the property or assets of the Borrower, other than the Mortgage and the Permitted Encumbrances;

5.6 The Financial data, reports, and other information furnished to Lender by the Borrower are accurate and complete and fairly present the financial position of the Borrower.

5.7 There has been no material adverse change in the condition, financial or otherwise, of the Borrower since the date of the most recent financial statement referred in Section 5.6;

5.8 To the best of Borrower's knowledge, there is no action, suit or proceeding at law or in equity or by or before any governmental instrumentality or other agency now pending or, to the knowledge of the Borrower, threatened against or affecting the Borrower which, if adversely determined, would have a material adverse effect on the business, operations, properties (including the Mortgaged Property), assets or condition, financial or otherwise of the Borrower;

5.9 The Borrower has obtained or will cause to be obtained all necessary governmental permits for the Project; and the dwellings on the Mortgaged Property after completion of the Project will comply with all applicable building, zoning, subdivision, landuse, health, historic preservation, licensing, rent control, planning, sanitation, architectural access, lead paint removal, and all applicable environmental protection ordinances, regulations or laws;

5.10 To the best of Borrower's knowledge, there are no defaults or sets of facts which, with the passage of time or otherwise, would constitute a default (i) under any agreements by and between the Borrower and the lenders providing the Junior Financing, (ii) under this Agreement or any other Loan Documents, (iii) or under the organizational documents of the Borrower; and

5.11 The proceeds of the Loan and the Junior Financing, and any other sources of funds disclosed by the Borrower to the Lender, provide sufficient funds to complete and operate the Project in accordance with the provisions and requirements of this Agreement.

Each of the foregoing representations, warranties, and covenants survives the making of the Loan and any advance of funds pursuant to this Agreement.

SECTION 6. BORROWER'S COVENANTS

During the term of the Loan, the Borrower shall comply with all of the terms and conditions of the Loan Documents, and the Borrower shall:

6.1 Commence and diligently and continuously continue construction of the Project in a timely manner and in accordance with the Project Schedule and the Project Budget, and substantially in accordance with the Plans and Specifications.

6.2 Construct the Project in compliance with all applicable laws, regulations, codes and ordinances. The Borrower shall notify the Lender when the Project is complete; and provide to the Lender certifications or documentation as reasonably necessary to establish the following:

- (i) certificates of occupancy have been issued for all units in the Project;
- (ii) a certificate has been executed by the architect for the Project stating that the Mortgaged Property complies with all applicable laws, codes, ordinances and regulations; and
- (iii) all funds advanced under this Agreement were expended for Eligible Project Costs.

6.3 Operate the Project in accordance with provisions of the Mortgage and the other Loan Documents.

6.4 Continuously comply with (i) all applicable building, fire, licensing, health, sanitation, historic preservation, environmental protection, rent control, landuse, subdivision and zoning ordinances and regulations promulgated by any national, state or local governmental body, agency, or division having jurisdiction over the Mortgaged Property, (ii) the organizational documents of the Borrower, and (iii) all restrictions or other encumbrances affecting title to the Mortgaged Property. The Borrower shall comply with the applicable requirements of the national and local boards of the fire underwriters and furnish to the Lender such evidence of compliance as the Lender may reasonably require.

6.5 Keep proper and separate books of account and make, or cause to be made, full and true entries of all dealings and transactions of every kind relating to the Mortgaged Property, which books and records are to be open to inspection by the Lender, its agents and representatives upon at least forty-eight (48) hours' notice and during the hours of 9:00 a.m. to 5:00 p.m. Monday through Friday at the Mortgaged Property or at the Borrower's principal office within the State of ~~Georgia~~ Florida.

6.6 Furnish the Lender with such reports, financial statements, records and other information relating to the financial condition or operations of the Borrower and the construction and operation of the Project, as the Lender may reasonably require, including, but not limited to, (i) annual audited financial statements of the Borrower (to be delivered to the Lender within one hundred twenty (120) days of the end of Borrower's fiscal year), and (ii) such other reports to show that the Project is being built and operated consistently with this Agreement, the organizational documents of the Borrower, and the other Loan Documents.

6.7 Perform all its obligations and agreements under the loan documents executed in connection with the Junior Financing, the organizational documents of the Borrower, and any other agreements or instruments to which the Borrower is a party, and which relate to the Loan or to the Project. The Borrower shall give notice to the Lender of any notices received by it from any lender providing the Junior Financing relative to any default or delinquency under the Junior Financing. The Borrower shall not increase the amount of, amend, terminate, renew, extend, or refinance the Junior Financing, without the prior written consent of the Lender, which consent the Lender shall not unreasonably withhold, condition, or delay.

6.8 Promptly before they expire, renew all licenses or other permits required for operation of the Project, and provide copies of the same to the Lender no later than ~~ten (10)~~ fourteen (14) days after receipt.

6.9 From and after completion of the Project, provide and operate ___________ (___) rental housing units on the Mortgaged Property.

6.10 Use Loan proceeds solely for Eligible Project Costs included and ensure that the proceeds of the Loan are not to be re-loaned or assigned to any party and are not to be used for any purpose prohibited by the Loan Documents.

6.11 Upon request and subject to zoning or other land use regulation, permit a sign no larger than three (3) feet square to be erected on the ground not the building on Mortgaged Property at a location selected by the Lender indicating that the Mortgaged Property is being financed in part by the Lender.

6.12 Not amend or modify the Borrower's articles of organization or bylaws without the Lender's prior written consent, which consent the Lender shall not unreasonably withhold, condition, or delay.

6.13 Until completion of the Project, cause to be maintained in full force and effect a policy or policies of builder's risk completed value insurance with fire, earthquake, and extended coverage, all in such form and in such amounts as the Lender from time to time reasonably requires.

SECTION 7. EVENTS OF DEFAULT

The occurrence of any one or more of the following events constitutes an "Event of Default" under the terms of this Agreement:

7.1 The Borrower assigns this Agreement or any money advanced under this Agreement or any interest in this Agreement or if any interest of the Borrower in the Mortgaged Property is terminated, sold, conveyed, or otherwise transferred, without the prior written consent of the Lender (excluding the replacement of equipment by the Borrower), which consent the Lender shall not unreasonably withhold, condition, or delay.

7.2 Any representation or warranty made in this Agreement or in any report, certificate, financial statement or other instrument furnished in connection with this Agreement or the Loan proves to be false in any material respect as of the date given.

7.3 The Borrower fails to pay the principal of, or fees or interest on, the Note or any other indebtedness of the Borrower under the Loan Documents after the same is due and payable and such failure continues beyond the date which is ten (10) days after written demand is made by the Lender.

7.4 The Borrower defaults in the due observance or performance of any other covenant, condition or agreement to be observed or performed by the Borrower pursuant to the terms of any of the Loan Documents and such default remains uncured thirty (30) days after written notice is given by the Lender to the Borrower; provided, however, that if the curing of such default cannot reasonably be accomplished with due diligence within said period of thirty (30) days, then the Borrower has such additional reasonable period of time to cure such default as may be necessary, not to exceed an additional ninety (90) days, so long as: (i) the Borrower has commenced to cure such default within said thirty (30) day period and diligently prosecutes such cure to completion and (ii) the Lender does not deem the Mortgaged Property jeopardized by such further delay.

7.5 The Borrower (i) applies for or consents to the appointment of a receiver, trustee, or liquidator of the Mortgaged Property, (ii) admits in writing its inability to pay its debts as they mature, (iii) makes a general assignment for the benefit of creditors, or (iv) is adjudicated a bankrupt or insolvent (however such insolvency may be evidenced).

7.6 Any proceeding involving the Borrower is commenced by or against the Borrower under any bankruptcy or reorganization arrangement, probate, insolvency, readjustment of debt, dissolution, or liquidation law of the United States, or any state, but if such proceedings are instituted no Event of Default occurs under this Agreement unless the Borrower either approves, consents to, or acquiesces in such proceedings, or such proceedings are not dismissed no later than ~~sixty (60)~~ ninety (90) days after they were commenced.

7.7 An order, judgment, or decree is entered, without the application, approval, or consent of the Borrower, by any court of competent jurisdiction approving a petition seeking reorganization or approving the appointment of a receiver, trustee or liquidator of the Borrower or all or a substantial part of its assets, and such order, judgment, or decree continues unstayed and in effect for a period of ~~sixty (60)~~ ninety (90) days after it was entered.

7.8 Any change in the legal form of, or the beneficial interest in the Borrower or either of its participants, except for an intra-family transfer of beneficial interest, or the termination or dissolution of the Borrower.

7.9 Any judgment, warrant, writ of attachment, or any similar process (in an amount exceeding ~~$10,000~~ $50,000, or, if more than one action, when added together all such actions exceed ~~$10,000~~ $50,000) is issued or filed against the Borrower or against property or assets of the same, and is not vacated, bonded, or stayed or satisfied within ~~sixty (60)~~ ninety (90) days.

7.10 Failure on the part of the Borrower, continuing beyond any applicable grace or cure period, in the due observance or performance of any other covenant, condition or agreement to be observed or performed pursuant to the loan documents executed in connection with the Junior Financing, or any other mortgage note or any documents or instruments now or hereafter existing entered into by the Borrower and secured by the Mortgaged Property.

SECTION 8. RIGHTS ON DEFAULT

Upon the occurrence of any one or more of the Events of Default enumerated in the foregoing Section 7, and at any time thereafter, then:

8.1 The Lender may declare all indebtedness due under the Note and any and all other indebtedness of the Borrower to the Lender due under the other Loan Documents or otherwise to be due and payable, whether or not the indebtedness evidenced by the Note or the other Loan Documents is otherwise due and payable and whether or not the Lender has initiated any foreclosure or other action for the enforcement pursuant to the provisions of the Loan Documents, whereupon all indebtedness due under the Note and the other Loan Documents and any other such indebtedness becomes forthwith due and payable, both as to principal and interest, without presentment, demand, protest or notice of any kind, all of which are expressly waived by the Borrower.

8.2 For the purposes of carrying out the provisions and exercising the rights, powers and privileges granted by this Section 8, the Borrower hereby irrevocably constitutes and appoints the Lender its true and lawful attorneyinfact with full power of substitution, to execute, acknowledge, and deliver any instruments and to perform any acts which are referred to in this Section 8, in the name and on behalf of the Borrower. The power vested in said attorneyinfact is coupled with an interest and irrevocable.

8.3 Upon the occurrence of any of said Events of Default, the Lender may exercise the rights, powers, and privileges provided in this Section 8 and all other remedies available to the Lender under this Agreement or under any of the other Loan Documents or at law or in equity, including but not limited to the commencement of foreclosure proceedings under the Mortgage, the right to cure Borrower's defaults as more fully set forth in the Mortgage or the commencement of an action seeking specific performance under any Loan Documents, whether or not the indebtedness evidenced and secured by the Loan Documents or otherwise is due and payable, and whether or not the Lender has instituted any foreclosure proceedings or other action for the enforcement of its rights under any of the Loan Documents. Failure of the Lender to exercise any rights or remedies at any time does not constitute a waiver of any of the rights or remedies of the Lender.

SECTION 9. MISCELLANEOUS

9.1 The Borrower shall not assign or attempt to assign directly or indirectly, any of its rights under this Agreement or under any instrument referred to in this Agreement without the prior written consent of the Lender in each instance, <u>which consent the Lender shall not unreasonably withhold, condition, or delay</u>. Any assignee or purported assignee is bound by all the terms of the assigned documents.

9.2 The Borrower and the Lender shall provide any notice, request, instruction or other document to be given under this Agreement to each other in writing and delivered personally or sent by certified or registered mail, postage prepaid, to the addresses set forth in below. Either party may change the address(es) to which notices are to be sent to such party by giving written notice of such change of address to the other party in the manner provided for giving notice. Any such notice, request, instruction, or other document is conclusively deemed to have been received and be effective on the day on which personally delivered or, if sent by certified or registered mail, on the day on which mailed. Lender shall use reasonable efforts to send courtesy copies of all notices sent to Borrower to Borrower's counsel at the address set forth below, provided that any failure to send such a courtesy copy shall not affect the validity of any notice:

If to Borrower:

____

____

____

____

Attention: ____________________

With a courtesy copy to:

____

____

____

____

Attention: ____________________

If to Lender:

____

____

____

____

Attention: ____________________

With a courtesy copy to:

____

____

____

____

Attention: ____________________

9.3 The Loan Documents are governed by the laws of the State of Georgia. Georgia choice of law principles apply to the interpretation of this provision.

9.4 No modification or waiver of any provision of the Loan Documents, nor consent to any departure by the Borrower from the Loan Documents is effective unless the same is in writing, and then such waiver or consent is effective only in the specific instance and for the purpose for which given. No failure or delay on the part of the Lender in exercising any right, power, or privilege under this Agreement or under the Note or the Loan Documents operates as a waiver under such documents, nor does single or partial exercise of such waiver preclude any other or further exercise or the exercise of any other right, power, or privilege.

9.5 This Agreement and all covenants, agreements, representations, and warranties made in this Agreement survive the making by the Lender of the Loan and the execution and delivery to the Lender of the Loan Documents, and the completion of the Project, and continue in full force and effect so long as the Note is outstanding and unpaid. This Agreement inures to the benefit of and is binding on the successors and assigns of the Lender and the permitted successors and assigns of the Borrower.

9.6 All Exhibits referred to in this Agreement are by such references fully incorporated into this Agreement.

The Lender and the Borrower have each duly executed, or caused to be duly executed, this Agreement in the name and behalf of each of them (acting by their respective officers or appropriate legal representatives, as the case may be, duly authorized) as of the day and year first above written.

BORROWER:

____

By: __________________________

By: __________________________

Name:

Title:

LENDER: ______________________

By: ___________________________
Name:
Title:

Exhibit A: Property Description
Exhibit B: Plans and Specifications
Exhibit C: Project Budget
Exhibit D: Project Schedule

www.ingramcontent.com/pod-product-compliance
Lightning Source LLC
LaVergne TN
LVHW022043200926
848481LV00003B/760